MONEYNOMICS

MONEYNOMICS

THE EVOLUTION OF MONEY IN THEORY, PRACTICE, AND POLICY

STEVEN RICCHIUTO

GREENLEAF
BOOK GROUP PRESS

This publication is designed to provide accurate and authoritative information in regard to the subject matter covered. It is sold with the understanding that the publisher and author are not engaged in rendering professional services. If expert assistance is required, the services of a competent professional should be sought.

Published by Greenleaf Book Group Press
Austin, Texas
www.gbgpress.com

Distributed by Greenleaf Book Group

For ordering information or special discounts for bulk purchases, please contact Greenleaf Book Group at PO Box 91869, Austin, TX 78709, 512.891.6100.

Design and composition by Greenleaf Book Group and Sheila Parr
Cover design by Greenleaf Book Group and Sheila Parr
©iStockphoto.com/zentilia

Publisher's Cataloging-in-Publication data is available.

Print ISBN: 978-1-62634-716-8

eBook ISBN: 978-1-62634-717-5

Part of the Tree Neutral® program, which offsets the number of trees consumed in the production and printing of this book by taking proactive steps, such as planting trees in direct proportion to the number of trees used: www.treeneutral.com

Printed in the United States of America on acid-free paper

20 21 22 23 24 25 26 10 9 8 7 6 5 4 3 2 1

First Edition

Contents

Preface

The evolution of macroeconomic thinking since the Great Depression can be divided into three major periods: (1) the Keynesian period; (2) the monetarist period; and (3) the New Keynesian period. Money plays a unique role in each of these theories of how the economy functions and, as a result, so does monetary policy. However, instead of focusing only on the Fed, as most modern macro studies tend to do, this book will review money: its role in the economy; the different forms it has taken; the different monetary systems that have been employed domestically; the role of the reserve currency; and how currency valuations are determined, at least in theory.

The intent is to fill in the missing pieces in a literature rich in analyses of the Fed and its role in controlling money, interest rates, and the economy, but which is limited in analyzing a primary target of Fed policy and macro modeling. By expanding the reader's familiarity with the role of money and its history, a greater appreciation of today's global deflation risks can be gained. Additionally, the reader will better understand why the cryptocurrency craze fizzled and why Modern Monetary Theory is being discussed seriously in policy circles.

Acknowledgments

A number of colleagues and old friends deserve to be identified for their contribution to this study of the evolution of money's role in the economy in theory, in practice, and in policy. Specifically, the work of Tetsuo "Harry" Ishihara needs to be recognized. Harry's organizational skills, dedication, and research abilities were truly invaluable in compiling the information necessary to complete this study. The editing skills of a dear friend, Seton Seremba-Brown, also need to be highlighted. Seton has been my go-to person for years, and she has never let me down. Special thanks to the management of Mizuho Securities USA LLC for indulging my repeated desire to dig into our country's economic history and explore the lessons history can teach us about the future. My thanks also go to Kurt Switala for his fast compliance review and content suggestions and to Daniel Poole, Mizuho's editor, for his fast and precise proofreading of my initial drafts. I would like to thank my family for their support, patience, and understanding. Finally, the coordination skills of Ashley Horne also need to be mentioned, as they always amaze me.

Introduction

Money is central to the underlying workings of the economy. Its creation dramatically expanded commerce even in early civilizations, while the ability to debase its value has plagued every monetary system ever created. Money provides three essential services to society: It smooths transactions; it is the unit of account against which value can be measured; and it serves as a store of value. Explaining why people hold or demand money balances has led to many theories, most of which rely on the transaction services provided by money, but the strong desire among its holders to avoid any devaluation suggests that the store of value service is also central to its value. This alternative view sees money as one of the many financial assets held by individuals and corporations looking to maximize the return on their accumulated assets over time. In the search for a monetary system, that retains the purchasing power of the currency employed, there has been a strong tendency for precious metals or other collectibles to serve as the monetary asset.

The benefits of commodity/metallic money are that their supply is limited and individuals desire them for their intrinsic value, as well as the transaction services provided. The discipline imposed on the economy by a gold standard is both a key benefit and a major weakness. Because the supply of gold in the economy is fixed at any one point in time, it limits how rapidly the economy can expand. At times, this limitation has led to undesired unemployment and deflation in addition to a redistribution of wealth from lender to borrower. These negative aspects, in turn, create an incentive for governments to debase their currencies and drive down the relative value of the currency over time.

A trade-off between a discipline imposed by a gold standard on a monetary regime and a limitation imposed on short-term growth has led to repeated attempts by governments to modify a gold-based monetary standard. The idea is that by relaxing some of the restrictions imposed by a precious metal standard, the benefits of a disciplined approach can be maintained while avoiding any major drawbacks. A gold reserve standard and a gold exchange standard are two of the modifications that have been tried, and, in the end, failed to deliver the desired results. The most famous of these attempts was the post–World War II monetary regime generally known as Bretton Woods. This system created the International Monetary Fund (IMF) and the World Bank to administer a system of fixed exchange rates tied to gold with the US dollar as the international reserve currency.

The motivation behind the US Treasury Department's desire to establish a stable postwar monetary framework for the free world was to avoid a repeat of the economic conditions that helped precipitate both World War I and World War II.

Specifically, the Bretton Woods framework was designed to avoid competitive devaluations. Currency stability was seen as essential for increased trade and a broad-based rise in living standards typically associated with the increased specialization that trade allows. So that this new system could function properly, domestic policy makers at the time, unfortunately, needed to undertake fiscal and monetary policy action that benefited other members of the system over the domestic economy. Not surprisingly, this turned out to be politically more difficult to do in practice than in theory.

Conflicts of interest began to surface early on, as Western Europe and Japan began to run trade surpluses while the domestic economy began to lose the competitive advantage that existed immediately after World War II. The dollar's central role in the Bretton Woods system was a key contributor to this shift in trade dynamics, as the demand for dollars increased its relative value. A progressive domestic policy agenda undertaken by President Johnson and the expanded US military role during the Cold War required that interest rates remain low, even as fiscal policy and demographic shifts stretched the economy's limits and that of the currency regime established at Bretton Woods. The result was rapidly rising prices and a declining currency, both of which added to the growing trade imbalance that consistently favored overseas manufacturers at the expense of domestic companies and workers.

The inherent weaknesses in the system were most evident in the divergence between the market's price for gold and the official price set by the Treasury. This divergence in the price of gold reflected the relative acceleration in domestic inflation, which led to a run on the gold supply as other central banks took advantage of the gold spread. Eventually, the pressures on the gold stock became too great, and President Nixon was forced to close the gold window in 1971, technically ending Bretton Woods and establishing a free-floating fiat currency standard. Although this solved the immediate currency crisis, domestic economic imbalances persisted as policy makers continued to stress the economy's growth limits for short-term political gains associated with low unemployment. As a result, economists' worst fears were realized—inflation spiraled out of control under a fiat monetary standard.

As domestic economic imbalances continued to grow, and an inflation psychology became embedded in the economy, the unanticipated dynamic of stagflation developed. This politically unacceptable development, characterized by simultaneously accelerating inflation and rising unemployment, created the next economic crisis as the dollar plunged. The decline in the dollar established a negative feedback loop, helping power the inflation spiral, and instigated the first major shift in economic thinking since Keynes penned *The General Theory of Employment, Interest and Money* in 1936.

In the shadow of stagflation and the currency crises it triggered, which destabilized the global economy, the Federal Reserve (Fed) shifted course and embraced the economic principles advanced by a new breed of economists, called monetarists, led by Milton Friedman and Anna Schwartz. Instead of targeting interest rates to support fiscal policy, as championed by Keynes, who saw unemployment and deflation as the greatest risk facing an economy, the monetarists focused on controlling inflation as the means of ensuring maximum long-term economic growth. The role of the Fed in the monetarists' world was to target a rate of growth in money. By injecting just enough liquidity into the economy to support real growth without generating inflation, the economy would, over the long term, maximize employment. A little inflation was still seen as necessary for a smooth-functioning economy, but just enough that inflation no longer entered the decision-making process of the private sector.

This new approach was based primarily on the empirical evidence showing that inflation was highly correlated with money growth over the long run but not with real growth. As such, any trade-off that existed between money growth and the real economy was just temporary, and in the end, inflationary. This new approach unhinged interest rates from monetary policy and allowed short rates to be determined by market dynamics. The resulting spike in interest rates associated with the Fed's limiting liquidity in the banking industry in order to rein in money growth helped break the wage-price spiral at the heart of stagflation.

The spike in interest rates orchestrated by the Fed in order to limit money growth also initiated an acceleration in financial innovation that quickly altered the relationship between money and the economy. As individuals and corporations strived to economize on money balances in the wake of high and rising interest rates, banks pushed into new liabilities that paid interest on money balances held by depositors. Without these innovations, the banking industry's deposit base would have shrunk, and along with it, the economy's ability to grow. These new financial products blurred the lines between transactions and saving balances, rendering traditional measures of money useless from a monetary policy perspective. After a brief period of experimenting with targeting different monetary aggregates, the Fed abandoned its experiment with monetarism in April 1993; and a third school of economics thought relating to money and monetary policy was adopted: Neo-Keynesianism.

The third approach to economics adopted in the postwar period is arguably still in place today, though our analysis suggests that its value has faded, and it will need to be replaced very soon by yet another new approach, such as inflation targeting. The Neo-Keynesian approach returned the focus of monetary policy to targeting interest rates, bringing policy back to where it began in the 1940s—but this time, with a fiat monetary regime. The primary emphasis of the Fed in a Neo-Keynesian world is to ensure that the hard-fought gains made in controlling inflation under Chairman Paul Volcker are maintained by a more proactive monetary policy focus of controlling inflation, not sustaining the business cycle. This new emphasis has proven to be effective in keeping inflation under control and out of private-sector decision making through the last three business cycles. But in the wake of the 2007–2008 financial crisis, a new and potentially more daunting development has surfaced—the risk of deflation. The fact that deflation has become an important economic concern in a world of fiat currencies, where the Fed and other central banks have dramatically expanded their balance sheets, can only be explained by a shift in the global economy from a world of excess demand to that of excess supply. This fundamental transition in the economy has had far-reaching effects on the nature of the business cycle and the tools needed for policy makers to employ and ensure a healthy economic environment.

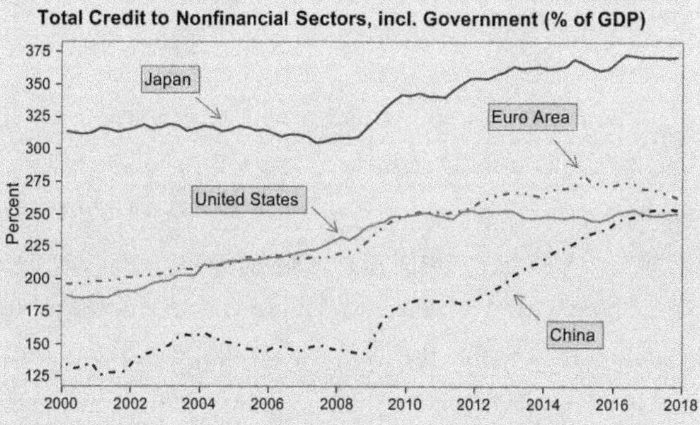

fig Introduction 1

Source: IMF, Macrobond, and Mizuho Securities USA

Total Credit to Nonfinancial Sectors (History of Debt to GDP for a Select Group of Countries)

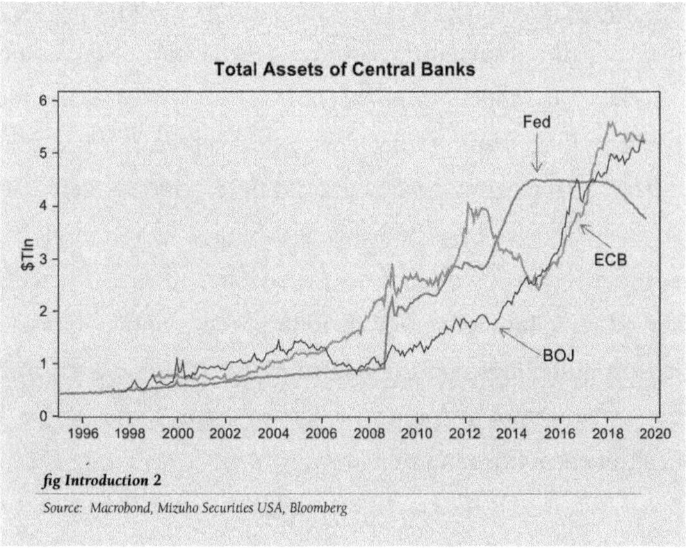

Total Assets of Central Banks (History of Central Bank Balance Sheets for These Same Countries)

Deflation is a more daunting problem for the economy than inflation; and, when it is coupled with excess supply, the results can be devastating. The best example of the adverse social consequences of deflation can be seen in the deep economic contraction associated with the Great Depression. It is important to note that the Depression did not end until World War II intervened, despite the application of progressive policies under Franklin D. Roosevelt's New Deal. Moreover, the deflation associated with a commodity or gold standard tends to self-correct as economic imbalances adjust due to the inflow or outflow of gold from the economy through the global market. In a fiat currency world, however, these imbalances tend not to correct themselves and deflation becomes embedded in the decision-making psychology.

The difficulty in exiting deflation once it gets established can easily be seen by looking at the Japanese experience since the 1990s real estate bubble burst. Despite extensive fiscal policy stimulus that has pushed the level of debt outstanding to upwards of 375 percent of GDP, Japan remains stuck in deflation. Besides an expansive fiscal policy, the Bank of Japan (BOJ) has also expanded its balance sheet by more than 940 percent to $5.2 trillion, and yet there is no evidence that the grip deflation has on the economy has dissipated. Although government programs designed to avoid widespread unemployment have limited the social costs of deflation in Japan, deflation has eroded sentiment and drained the economy of its strength, as workers have come to anticipate declining wages and prices.

Since the financial crisis in 2007–2008, Europe has been struggling with deflation as well. Deflation's grip on Europe reflects repeated economic shocks to the region's economy, first in 2011–2012, as the value of sovereign debt in the region got hammered by a spike in default risk among some smaller European countries. Then the record-high oil prices of 2014 further weakened the European economy; and, when oil prices plunged in 2015–2016, European banks got caught in the financial turbulence that followed. These repeated economic and financial market shocks, combined with the limits on fiscal policy imposed by the European Economic and Monetary Union (EMU), left the European Central Bank (ECB) as the only defense against global excess supply and deflation. Despite aggressive action by the ECB, it has become clear that monetary policy designed to control inflation is no match for deflation, even with a fiat currency. These accumulating deflation pressures have resulted in exceptionally low interest rates; and yet, near-zero rates have provided very little stimulus, suggesting a classical Keynesian liquidity trap may be at work.

Although the US economy has fared better than Japan or Europe in the latest business cycle, there is a risk that the domestic economy could succumb to the same global excess supply pressures that have pulled these other powerful economies down into a deflationary hole. To avoid this fate, it appears that the Fed needs to give up on the Neo-Keynesian model of gradual, preemptive interest rate adjustments. In fact, the growing dialogue surrounding MMT, or Modern Monetary Theory, is a direct result of the need for policy makers to think outside the box as traditional policy tools become less effective. Even though the economy has managed to pull together the longest expansion in the postwar period, the social pressures created by the demand for double-digit investment returns in a deflationary world have led to stagnant wages, reduced employment options, and the social pressures associated with limited wage gains for a growing portion of the working population. The increased concentration of wealth adds another layer to the unacceptable dynamic at work in the economy. Even the search for a new alternative monetary model can be seen in the cryptocurrency craze. The perceived debasement of the currency, as a result of the large-scale asset purchase programs initiated by the Fed and other central banks, has reduced confidence in the ability of policy makers to correct the economic imbalances generated by a world of excess supply and a fiat currency regime.

The dynamic forces at work in this economy and those highlighted above will be analyzed in detail in the following chapters. We will trace the evolution of money and the role of monetary policies both in theory and in practice. We will trace the evolution of money's role in the macroeconomic theory, starting with the groundbreaking work of Keynes and ending with a discussion of MMT. In the process, we will address the strengths and weaknesses of the Keynesian model, the monetarist alternative, and the Neo-Keynesian model that followed and is still being implemented, even though there is a growing body of evidence that even this model has reached its limits.

The origins of money in very early civilizations will then set the stage for a detailed discussion of the rich history of the various forms of money utilized even in this country, despite its relatively brief history. We will trace money from wampum to Bitcoin, with a good deal of emphasis on gold and the various metallic standards utilized until today's free-floating fiat currency mode was implemented in the early 1970s. Each form of money will be analyzed for its strengths and weaknesses. Through the evolution of money, it will be seen that the perfect form of currency and associated monetary policy still eludes us today, despite significant advances in empirical analysis, data availability, and decades of academic investigations. This analysis of money will explain why we are back to a situation where deflation is the greatest threat facing economies almost a century after the Great Depression, despite all that we have learned about the workings of the economy and the advanced statistical analysis available to economists and policy makers in a world of cheap computing power. The key lesson to be gleaned is that the economy is always evolving, as are tastes and preferences; as a result, economic models need to be continuously evaluated and modified in order for policy makers to stay relevant in a dynamic world.

Section 1

The Theoretical Role of Money in the Economy

Chapter 1

The Keynesian IS–LM Model

Money plays a central role in macroeconomic theory. In this chapter, we examine the first highly influential model of the economy where money was a key policy lever that could be manipulated to move an economy from one short-term equilibrium to another.

The genesis of this model can be traced to the work done by John Maynard Keynes during the late stages of the Great Depression (1929–1939) and presented in his *General Theory of Employment, Interest Rates and Money* published in 1936. According to Keynes's work, the Depression was caused by a widespread loss of confidence that led to underconsumption. Once panic and deflation set in, many people believed they could avoid further losses by steering clear of markets. Holding money became profitable as the price of goods and services dropped, suggesting that holding cash could allow individuals to buy more later. This dynamic became known as the *Keynesian Liquidity Trap*.

The macro dynamic outlined by Keynes in his *General Theory* was further developed by John Hicks in 1937 and later extended by Alvin Hansen into the mathematical model that would become the framework behind the macroeconomic theory between the 1940s and the 1970s, and is still the backbone of most introductory macroeconomics textbooks. The IS–LM model, or Hicks-Hansen model, shows the relationship between interest rates and real income that brings both markets for goods and services into alignment with those that are consistent with equilibrium in the liquidity market. The equilibrium in the liquidity market is dependent on the level of money provided to the economy by the Federal Reserve. As such, the IS–LM model shows that monetary policy could be exploited just as easily as fiscal policy for countercyclical purposes.

Basic Model Framework

The model is presented graphically as the intersection of two curves. One curve identifies the pairs of income and interest rates that identify possible equilibrium conditions in the market for goods and services, and the other identifies the conditions for equilibrium in the liquidity market. The level of income and interest rates that satisfies both markets simultaneously is the estimated short-term equilibrium for the economy. The IS (investment-saving) curve identifies pairs of income and interest rates that will result in equilibrium in the goods and services market. The equilibrium position is defined as the point where savings equals investment in the economy. When working through the various pairs of income and interest rates that satisfy the demand for consumer and investment goods under an equilibrium condition, the savings rate needs to equal investment so a downward-sloping IS curve is traced out.

The LM, or liquidity curve, determines the income and interest-rate pairs that satisfy the condition that demand for money equals the supply of money in the economy. The intersection between the downward-sloping IS curve and the upward-sloping LM curve is seen as the short-term equilibrium of the economy. Movement from one equilibrium to another can be generated by a policy-induced shift in either the IS or the LM curve. This will result in a different equilibrium pair of income and interest rates for the economy. Because we are considering short-term equilibrium, inflation is seen as having a limited effect on the economy, and the equilibrium pairs of income and interest rates are identified as real, or inflation adjusted, rather than nominal. To better understand this model, a brief but thorough discussion of the determinants of the IS and LM curve will prove useful and allow us to better understand the central role money plays in how the economy works, without getting overly technical.

Equilibrium in the Goods Market

The IS curve is a simple statistical model that depicts the level of real interest rates and real GDP or aggregate income that generate equilibrium in the markets for goods and services.

These interest-rate and aggregate income pairs satisfy the following equation, subject to the equilibrium condition that savings equals investment:

$$Y = C(Y - T(y)) + I(R, Y) + G$$

Here, Y represents real GDP and $C(Y - T(y))$ represents consumer spending as an increasing function of disposable income $(Y - T(Y))$; that is, the partial derivative of consumption with respect to disposable income is greater than zero. $I(R, Y)$ represents investment spending as a decreasing function of the real interest rate and an increasing function of real income; in other words, the partial derivatives of investment spending are negative for changes in real interest rates and positive for changes in real income. G represents government spending, which is set exogenously by the interaction of Congress and the administration. We could add a real asset variable as a positive determinant of consumer spending as well as net exports to the model, but for our purposes, these modifications are unnecessary. However, the difference between exports and imports would be a decreasing function of real income, or Y, since (1) the level of imports is positively related to real income; and (2) exports depend on factors outside this model.

The above equation can be rewritten as

$$S(Y - T(Y)) + T(Y) = I(R, Y) + G$$

S represents total savings and is a positive function of real income. In product market equilibrium, total savings (private plus government) must be equal to total investment including that undertaken by the government. The real income and interest-rate pairs that satisfy this equilibrium condition form the IS curve, or half of the Hicks-Hansen model of the macro economy. It should be noted that upward shifts in the IS curve can be generated by an increase in the relative desire to invest in new plant and equipment at any given level of interest rates, or by an increase in government spending. A reduction in the desire to consume for every dollar earned, or an increase in the desire to save, also shifts the IS curve upward and to the right; while a reduced sensitivity of investment to interest rates flattens the IS curve. The IS curve is not a complete model of equilibrium in the economy, in that it doesn't ensure equilibrium in liquidity markets, and therefore, in the labor market either. These will be discussed below.

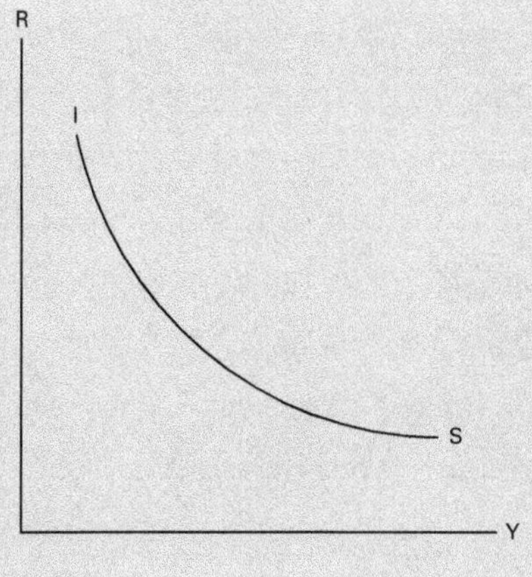

fig 1.1

IS Curve

Equilibrium in the Liquidity Markets

The LM curve shows the pairs of income and interest rates for which the money or liquidity market is in equilibrium, that is, where the demand and supply of money in the economy are in balance. This equilibrium curve is seen as upward sloping, representing the role of money and finance in the economy. Equilibrium in the liquidity market is determined by solving the following equation:

$$MS(R)/P = MD(Y, R) \text{ or } L(R) + K(Y)$$

MS(R) represents the supply of money provided to the economy by the Federal Reserve through the banking system. As rates rise, the banking industry tends to be more willing to provide additional loans to would-be borrowers and the supply of money to the economy increases through the level of demand deposits generated by banks. The aggregate price level in the economy is denoted by the letter *P*. It is essentially the price index that deflates nominal GDP to real GDP. Money demand, *MD(Y, R)*, can be interpreted as the sum of the speculative demand for money (which is negatively dependent on the level of interest rates) and the transactions demand of money (which is positively dependent on the level of income). As income in the economy tends to increase, the interest rates needed to keep the liquidity market in equilibrium tend to increase as well, giving the LM curve its positive slope.

The elasticity the LM curve exhibits depends on the sensitivity of the speculative demand for money to changes in interest rates. The flatter the speculative demand for money, the flatter the LM, and vice versa. Alternatively, the less sensitive the supply of money is to the level of interest rates, the more the LM curve shifts up and to the left. This equilibrium relationship shows the important role money plays in the economy, as it is key to the interaction between the product and money markets and can be manipulated to alter the level of aggregate demand in the economy. This will be seen more clearly in the following section.

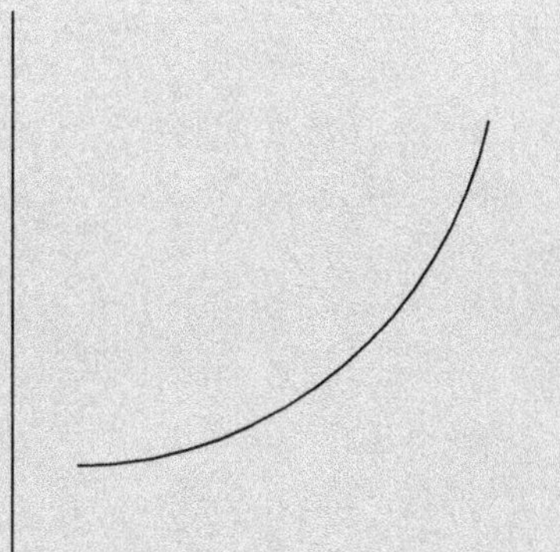

***fig* 1.2**

LM Curve

Product and Liquidity, Money Market Equilibrium

By simultaneously solving the IS and the LM equations for the level of output and interest rates that clear both markets, we get the level of real GDP that is associated with a given price level, or a single point on the aggregate demand curve. Also, note that *G*, government spending, and *P*, the aggregate price level, are two of the three exogenous variables in this model. Increasing *G* results in a higher level of output at a given level of prices. Increasing real money balances in the economy can accomplish a similar outcome of higher real GDP.

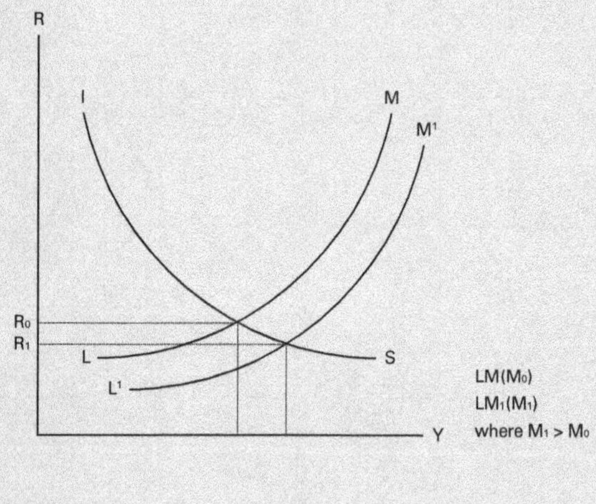

fig 1.3

IS–LM

Increasing or decreasing the aggregate price level, and calculating the equilibrium level of GDP consistent with equilibrium for the product and the liquidity markets, traces out an aggregate demand curve. By combining this aggregate demand relationship with an aggregate supply determined by the labor market condition (i.e., a Phillips curve), a complete model of the economy was constructed. This model became the basis behind all macroeconomic thinking in the postwar period, until it fell out of favor due to the era of stagflation that surfaced in the late 1970s and early 1980s. The labor market model was not capable of anticipating the changed dynamic between employment and inflation expectations that developed thirty years into the postwar period. This development required a new interpretation of how the economy functions. These new theories had to explain how prices could rise in an environment in which slack in the labor market was increasing (a rising jobless rate). This will be discussed in more detail in Chapter 3, Stagflation and the Rise of Monetarism.

Ascendance of Fiscal and Monetary Policy

The intuitive nature of the IS–LM aggregate demand/aggregate supply framework explains why policy makers relied heavily on this model from the 1940s through 1970s and even today, to some extent. For instance, the Trump/GOP Tax Cuts and

Jobs Act of 2017 is a modern-day example of trying to exploit the macro framework depicted by the Keynesian model to increase employment and lift the economy to a higher growth trajectory. The ease with which the various components of the model can be manipulated to simulate various macroeconomic and policy scenarios led to the belief among economists in the 1950s and 1960s that the business cycle could be dampened or even eliminated entirely with the right sequence of fiscal and monetary policy stimuli. The evolution of computers extended the life of the IS–LM framework, even when signs of the model's limitations began to surface. The Keynesian model identified by Hicks and Hansen could be easily modified to correct for certain errors, and the speed of computers in manipulating large data sets broadened the scope of the model to simulate results of policy changes not just at the sector level, but also at the industry and sub-industry level.

The Keynesian model, moreover, was the justification behind Roosevelt's New Deal programs enacted during the Depression. Programs like the Works Progress Administration (WPA) were the first concerted fiscal stimulus programs enacted. Unfortunately, it appears these early attempts at countercyclical policies were too small in scope to offset the monetary contraction that followed in the wake of some 9,000 Depression-era bank failures. The fact that Fed policy did not support the Roosevelt stimulus initiative is seen as a missed opportunity, and it shaped the postwar focus of monetary policy that emphasized controlling the level of interest rates in the economy as the means to maximizing growth and sustaining full employment. Essentially, monetary policy best serves the economy if it supports the fiscal policy decisions by elected officials by maintaining low short-term interest rates.

In the period following the conclusion of World War II, fiscal policy was used repeatedly to alter the trajectory of the economy. The so-called Kennedy tax cut enacted by President Johnson in 1964 is a well-publicized example of a Keynesian-inspired tax cut. At that time, the Fed saw its responsibility as supporting the macroeconomic decisions of the administration and Congress. The reported inelasticity of money supply during the Depression was broadly credited with having exacerbated the contraction in the economy and the deflationary spiral that followed. The Fed saw its role as amplifying and/or supporting the decisions made by elected policy makers. As such, the Fed concentrated its efforts on controlling the level of interest rates as the means for achieving its dual mandate of full employment and sustainable noninflationary real growth. This policy approach was fully consistent with the Keynesian IS–LM model outlined above.

By targeting the level of short-term interest rates that prevailed in the economy, individuals, households, and companies were able to make economic decisions with greater certainty. Confidence in the likely payoff of their investments would increase willingness to take risks and lift the economy. This policy approach would fall out of favor in the late 1970s but resurfaced in the wake of the 2007–2008 financial crisis. With an attempt to increase the willingness of economic agents to increase investment spending, the Fed aggressively lowered interest rates and established explicit guidance on how long policy would remain accommodative. In hindsight, this approach increased financial investment more than it increased physical investment, and the resulting asset inflation is another example of the model's misspecification.

Stagflation and the Demise of the Keynesian Model

The ultra-supportive role of monetary policy in the 1940s through the 1960s eventually created an inflation psychology that resulted in output growth becoming less responsive than inflation to repeated doses of fiscal policy stimulus. Over time, this inflation psychology resulted in the Phillips curve shifting laterally upward and eliminating the trade-off between prices and wages and the jobless rate. This dynamic altered the shape of the aggregate supply curve. The upward-sloping curve assumed in the IS–LM aggregate demand/aggregate supply model suggested workers had an increased desire to work as wages increased. The empirical evidence, however, revealed a much more vertical long-run aggregate supply curve.

The apparent divergence between the short-run and longer-run behavior of the aggregate demand and aggregate supply model depicted by Keynes set the stage for the stagflation of the late 1970s. Stagflation is an environment where unemployment rises even as wages and prices rise. This breakdown in the model would lead to a new brand of macro thinking advanced by economists such as Anna Schwartz and Milton Friedman. These so-called monetarists advocated a very different role for monetary policy in the economy (which we will discuss in the next chapter). What should already be clear from this overview of the Keynesian model is that money is a critical macroeconomic variable and deserves an in-depth understanding, both in theory and in practice. To this end, we will next discuss the theories behind the demand and supply of money.

Chapter 2

Demand and Supply of Money

The Keynesian short-term equilibrium model discussed in the previous chapter reveals the central role money plays in determining the level of income, interest rates, and prices that satisfy the overall equilibrium conditions of aggregate demand/aggregate supply in the economy. The demand for and the supply of money are one-half of the aggregate demand side of the equilibrium model developed by Keynes. A solid fundamental understanding of the liquidity market and its determinants will round out our understanding of the Keynesian model.

A thorough knowledge of the determinants of money demand and supply will also help our understanding of the macro dynamics that led to the demise of the Keynesian model and its replacement by the monetarist model championed by Milton Friedman and his contemporaries such as Anna Schwartz and George Stigler. These American economists theorized that in the long run only prices, not output, were affected by changing the supply of money in the economy. This new theory of general equilibrium can be modeled using the basic Keynesian IS–LM curve framework and can be modified to explain the stagflation environment of the late 1970s. This alternative view of the role of money in the economy will be explored in subsequent chapters, as well as the very different approaches to monetary policy it spawned.

In this chapter, we discuss the basic drivers for the demand and supply of money in order to provide the theoretical underpinnings of the liquidity market's equilibrium conditions illustrated in the IS–LM model. We will follow the basic discussion found in most macro textbooks regarding money demand and supply, which should rekindle old memories for those who have studied this topic before, and because it flows naturally from the work of Hicks and Hansen described in Chapter 1. Essentially, we will delve into the logic behind why money demand is positively affected by income and negatively affected by the level of interest rates in the economy. We will also look at the positive relationship between money supply and interest rates. This will provide a better understanding of the dynamic relationship between money demand and money supply at the heart of the Keynesian model. It will also allow us to dive into the important role the Federal Reserve plays, not only in this model but in the economy as well.

The Demand for Money

Economists generally divide the demand for real money balances into two components: a speculative component that is inversely related to real interest rates, and a transactions component that is positively related to real income or GDP and negatively related to real interest rates. This generalized model is a theoretical attempt to answer the question of why people hold money in a world where bonds earn interest and money doesn't. To answer this pivotal question, economists have developed four different theories, here described in the order in which they were developed.

The first approach to explaining why households and companies hold money balances is the *regressive expectations model* that is generally credited to Keynes. This theory says that people hold money when they expect bond prices to fall. In other words, people hold money when they expect interest rates to rise. Because individual expectations of whether interest rates are going to rise or fall (and by how much) varies widely, this theory tends to deliver a binary result at an individual level. Essentially, individuals will either hold all money or all bonds.

To address the shortfall in this first approach, economists next suggested that in an uncertain world where bond returns are unknown, and therefore risky, individuals would be best served holding both bonds and money. This model of money demand is referred to as the *portfolio approach*.

A third approach to the demand for money is the *inventory approach*. This theory suggests that there is a transaction need for holding money to smooth out the difference between an individual's stream of income and expenditures, and this depends critically on the level of real income. The higher the level of rates, or the greater the expected return on bonds, the smaller these transactional balances should be, given transaction costs.

The final approach suggests that *money is a consumer and producer good*, just like any other commodity. As a goods producer, businesses hold money to increase their efficiency in their financial transitions and are willing to forgo a little interest income for this efficiency. The same analysis holds true for an individual's demand for money. The higher the rate, the more willing companies and households will be to incur transaction costs. Money can also be viewed as any other good consumed in the economy. Households and businesses hold money because of the utility it provides in smoothing out the timing of expenditures and income stream, which is generally positively related to the level of income and negatively related to the level of short-term rates. Each of these approaches is discussed in more detail below.

Regressive Expectations Approach

The literature on this approach starts with investors' expected return on the bonds they hold. This return is composed of the coupon payment and its potential capital gain. The yield or coupon payment is fixed at the time of a bond's origination and is a stated percent of its face value. The real market rate of return is its coupon payment divided by its price. The capital gain is the expected percentage increase in the price of the bond from its purchase price. Combining these two components of the bondholders' return leads to the following equation:

e = r + r/r (expected) – 1

e = **real return expected on a bond**
r = **real market rate of return on a bond**
r (expected) = **long-term real rate of interest expected on a bond**

Since the return on holding money is zero, an individual will either hold all money or all bonds, depending on the return expected on holding bonds. This relationship between the individuals' demand for real money balances and the return expected on bonds can be depicted as a binary outcome:

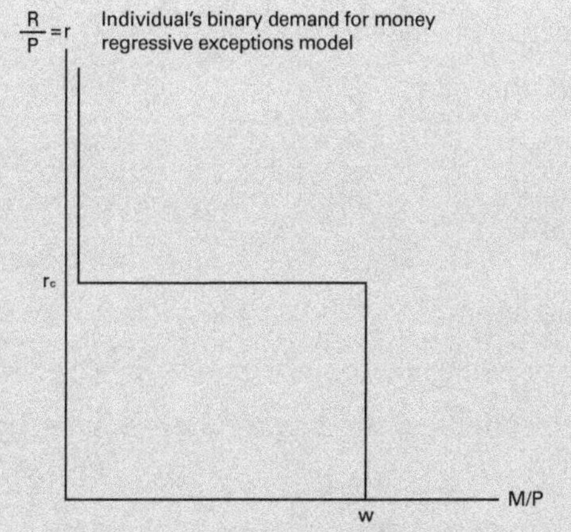

fig 2.1

Demand for Money

Specifically, this model suggests that an individual's demand for real money balances is zero at any interest rate above the equilibrium market rate of interest—and is 100 percent cash when rates are below the equilibrium rate. When rates are above the equilibrium level, the expected return on bonds is greater than zero; when rates are below this threshold level, the expected return on bonds will be negative and an individual would rather hold all cash.

Aggregating up from individuals' demand for money to that for the entire economy leads to a downward sloping or speculative demand for money, if we assume that individuals all have varying expectations concerning the direction of interest rates and an expected return on bonds. Essentially, there will be some level of interest rates above which no individual will hold cash and some rate low enough where everyone will want to hold only cash.

Portfolio Approach

The portfolio approach to the demand for money starts with the same expression for the real return expected on bonds. This approach builds on this framework by adding uncertainty into the model. The return expected on bonds is the combination of the bond's current return, or its coupon yield, and the capital gains expected. Uncertainty is added to the model by assuming that individuals are uncertain about the value of capital gains expected at any point in time, but they have some idea of the distribution of these gains around some critical value. Assuming the probabilities attached to different capital gains outcomes are distributed "normally," then the standard deviation of this bell-shaped distribution is a natural measure of the risk facing individuals in assessing their demand for money. The assumption of a normal distribution of returns suggests that there is a 66.7 percent chance that the actual return on holding bonds will fall in between the area under the bell-shaped curve defined by plus or minus one standard deviation around the mean return.

The expected return on holding bonds is the bond's current yield and its expected capital gain—suggesting that the expected total return from holding bonds for the individual is total dollars invested in bonds multiplied by the expected return on bonds, or

$$E(TR) = B \times (r + E(g))$$

$E(TR)$ = **expected real total return on bonds**
B = **dollar value invested in bonds**
r = **current real return or coupon yield**
$E(g)$ = **expected real capital gain from holding bonds**

The total risk associated with this portfolio is simply the dollar invested in bonds multiplied by the standard deviation of the expected capital gain on bonds:

$$STD(TR) = B \times STD(g)$$

STD(TR) = **standard deviation of the expected total return on holding bonds**
STD(g) = **standard deviation of expected capital gain from holding bonds**
B = **dollars invested in bonds**

These two equations can be solved simultaneously to show that the change in the expected total return on bonds with respect to changes in the total risk of this portfolio is equal to the expected return on a bond divided by the standard deviation of a bond's capital gain. The expected return on holding bonds is equal to the current yield and the expected capital gain. This relationship becomes the budget constraint applied to an individual's indifference to curves—between holding cash and/or bonds, depending on the riskiness of the individual's holdings and on the current return.

Assuming that individuals tend to be diversifiers, that is, they hold a portfolio of both bonds and cash by varying their current return on bonds, a diversifier will tend to hold cash as interest rates rise. Aggregating up over the entire population will yield a negatively sloped aggregate money demand curve. This portfolio approach provides a solid foundation for the speculative demand for money in the Keynesian model and explains why it is downward sloping. As such, it is now time to discuss the transactions model behind the demand for money.

Inventory Approach

The speculative demand for holding real money balances is not the only reason individuals hold cash. Economists theorize that the principal reason is to smooth out the timing differences between income streams and expenditures. The transaction motive is, therefore, directly related to a household's level of income. But because cash balances earn no interest, there is also an opportunity cost to holding income in cash. As such, transactional demand for money is also seen as being negatively related to the level of interest rates. The higher the level of interest rates, the greater the opportunity cost, and the more that households are economizing on their cash holdings. To add rigor to this intuitive approach, an interest-inelastic transactions model was developed by William Baumol, summarized as follows.

Suppose an individual is paid monthly and spends a total amount of real income, y, on purchases spread evenly throughout the month. The individual has the option of holding transaction balances in money or in bonds. Bonds yield a stated rate of interest, r, if held for a full month, and proportionally less if they are held for a shorter period. Bond transactions incur a cost, which prevent the person from continuously exchanging bonds into money as transactions are made. Accordingly, individuals will exchange most of their paycheck for bonds—more realistically an interest-earning bank account—and periodically withdraw funds to make cash purchases.

The more transactions an individual incurs, the longer the average bond holding period will be and the higher the interest rate earned. The more often an individual redeems bonds for cash, the larger the transaction costs accrued. As such, the number of transactions between bonds and cash an individual makes each month determines the trade-off between interest earned and the transaction cost accrued. Alternatively, think of this as minimizing the total cost of such transactions when interest rates and transaction costs are assumed to be known, and the opportunity cost of cash by not holding bonds is a substituted form of the interest earned:

$$m = (ay/2rT)^{1/2}$$

m = **average real money balances held**

a = **transaction cost per trade**

y = **real income**

r = **real interest rate paid on bonds or by banks**

T = **interval between paychecks**

This equation for the optimal level of money balances held clearly shows the positive relationship between real income and the negative relationship to real rates. To obtain an aggregate transactions demand for real money balances, all that is left is to sum up the individuals' demands for real money balances as income varies at each level of interest rates. Although the inventory approach explains the Keynes transactions demand for money, other economists have suggested that the demand for money should be viewed as the demand for any other good or service.

Money as a Consumer and Producer Good

The three money demand models already summarized have basically followed the Keynesian approach, where individuals opt to hold money balances for either transactional or speculative purposes. Milton Friedman, using a traditional microeconomic approach to modeling consumer and business behavior, suggested a more modern approach. This micro approach to macroeconomics postulates that individuals hold money because it yields a utility—the convenience of holding the means of payment rather than making frequent trips to the bank or broker and risking capital loss by holding bonds. Household demand for holding real money balances should be viewed like a consumer's demand for any other real consumer good and service. As such, the demand for real money balances should depend positively on real income and negatively on the return offered by other assets that could be used to store value.

Producers hold money as any other productive asset that can be used to smooth out payment and expenditure streams, just as their demand for real capital services depends on the level of real income and the relative return on other assets. As such, producers' demand for real money balances is also positively related to income and negatively to the rate of interest, given that an increase in the demand for bonds implies a reduction in the demand for money. This is essentially the general form of the money demand portion of the LM curve.

$$M/P = m = MD(y, r)$$

M = **nominal money balances**

P = **aggregate prices**

m = **real money balances**

MD = **money demand function**

y = **real income**

r = **real rate of interest**

These four separate approaches to modeling the demand for money are the basic workhorses of this area of research. However, to finish developing the IS–LM framework, we need to also develop a model of money supply to complete the liquidity market model discussed in Chapter 1. In doing so, the central role of the Federal Reserve and the banking system will also become apparent. For most consumers of financial media, the Fed's prominent role in the economy is evident, but many financial news listeners do not really understand the nature of the role played by the Fed. Hopefully, this next section will serve to inform or remind the readers of how the Fed fits into the broader discussion of macro equilibrium and the importance of money in determining aggregate income, interest rates, and prices in the economy.

Money Supply Model

There are many measures of money supply or monetary aggregates that can be calculated by adding up various bank liabilities available to households and producers in the economy. The measure of money that is most consistent with the Keynesian IS–LM model is a very narrow measure that consists of currency—defined as paper money and coins—in the hands of the nonbank public and checkable deposits in both the commercial banking system and other depository institutions such as savings and loan associations (S&Ls). This narrow set of liquid liabilities is differentiated from others in the economy: (1) they are generally accepted as a means of payment; and (2) they earn little or no interest.

This narrow measure was the most generally used definition of money supply until the 1980s, when the introduction of interest-bearing checking accounts and money market mutual funds blurred the lines between money balances and savings balances. The rapid growth in these innovative financial liabilities eventually forced economists to consider broader measures of money. Unfortunately, these alternative aggregates failed to maintain a stable relationship with the economy, and both reduced the value of the Keynesian model and diminished the value of Friedman's monetarist model that replaced Keynes's in the 1980s. This Keynes-to-Friedman transition will be detailed in the next chapter, as well as the post-monetarist model used today. To further develop the Keynesian IS–LM model in order to highlight the role of money and the Federal Reserve in the economy, we will continue to focus on the most liquid money measure: cash plus checkable deposits, or M1. Focusing on this monetary aggregate allows for a clear introduction to the linkage between Federal Reserve policy decisions and the supply of money available in the economy.

The makers of monetary policy can directly control the level of currency and coins in circulation by controlling its portfolio of US government-backed securities held on its balance sheet. The Fed also exercises a high degree of control over the level of checkable deposits created by deposit-taking financial institutions. The Fed's ability to influence the level of checkable deposits is tied to its regulatory role. Specifically, the Fed sets the banking system's reserve requirements. By requiring deposit-taking institutions to hold a fraction of the deposits they take in as protection against unanticipated withdrawals, the Fed sets the upper limit on how many checkable deposits can be created by the banking system. A reserve ratio of 5 percent sets a limit of twenty times the level of reserves the Fed injects into the economy for total checkable deposits. Presumably, profit-motivated banks will always desire to expand the money supply to its maximum through their lending decisions, which, in turn, will generate deposit liabilities. This is not the only process with which the Fed can control the level of money.

Fed open-market operations can be used to add or drain reserves from the banking system and directly influence deposit generation by banks. Bank reserves have been called *high-powered money* because reserves are the base from which banks can expand their deposit base, given a specific reserve ratio. The Fed adds reserves to the system by temporarily buying Treasury securities from primary dealers and their customers and can drain reserves by temporarily selling Treasury debt into the market. Besides these temporary additions and subtractions, the Fed can permanently add or subtract reserves from the banking system through outright purchase and sales of government-backed debt. One additional source of reserves to the banking system provided through the Federal Reserve is the discount window. The discount window is a vehicle for banks to temporarily borrow reserves from the Fed for a fee, or the discount rate.

The supply of reserves is critical to determining the level of money available in the economy at each level of the interest rate or level of the Fed funds rate. The Fed funds rate is the base rate for unsecured overnight lending between banks, and it forms the base rate for all other borrowing. The supply of reserves available to the banking system is set by the Federal Reserve. The makers of monetary policy inject a certain level of nonborrowed reserves into the system through the purchase of assets and the liabilities that they accrue. A big chunk of the Fed's assets are its holdings of Treasury securities and other government-backed debt held on its balance sheet, either permanently or temporarily. Beyond the level of nonborrower reserves are those the Fed provided through the discount window, as discussed earlier. The biggest liabilities on the Fed's balance sheet are the level of Federal Reserve notes circulating in the economy and stored in its bank vaults.

Discount window. Banks can borrow from the discount window under three separate programs offered by the Federal Reserve: primary credit program, secondary credit program, and seasonal credit. At this time, we are most interested in the primary credit program. It is typically an overnight loan to a healthy financial institution to help it better manage its reserve balances. The secondary credit program is designed for financial institutions that are experiencing a liquidity issue caused by a significant financial difficulty. This is a relatively new lending facility, which was part of a 2002 proposal to alter the way the discount window was administered. Seasonal credit is extended to small depositary institutions that have large recurring fluctuations in their funding, such as those experienced by banks in agricultural areas around planting and harvesting times.

The rate charged on a primary credit facility has changed throughout the years. It has gone from being a subsidized rate, at the time of Keynes and Friedman, to a penalty rate today. It was not until 2003 that the price attached to the primary credit facility was altered. Currently the primary credit discount rate is set at 100 basis points above the target Fed funds rate. From the time of Keynes to late 2003, banks could borrow from the Fed at a rate well below the funds rate. However, banks' willingness to borrow from the Fed has changed over time, as institutions became less and less willing to borrow, for fear of being perceived as having a liquidity issue.

For our purposes, let's assume that the discount rate remains a subsidy rate and that banks are opportunistic in their borrowing at the discount window. The rate charged on borrowing under the secondary credit facility is set at 50 basis points above the primary credit rate due to the risks involved, while seasonal borrowing at the discount window is set as an average of several financing rates.

Because the supply of nonborrowed reserves provided by the Fed tends to be fixed in the short run, it is the ability to borrow at the discount window that provides the interest rate elasticity to money supply in the Keynesian IS–LM model. As interest rates rise, banks become more willing to borrow at the discount window, and the level of reserves expands as well as money supply. The role of the Fed in supplying reserves to the banking system pushes the LM curve to the right and increases the level of equilibrium income in the economy:

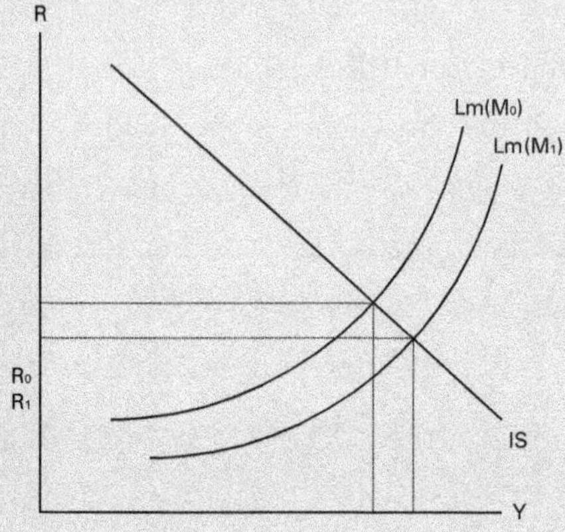

fig **2.2**

LM Shift $M_t 1 > M_0$

To this end, the LM equation developed by Hicks and Hansen is consistent with the workings of the banking industry and confirms that money supply is positively related to the level of interest rates because of the Fed's role as a lender as a last resort. Moreover, the important role of monetary policy in determining the short-term equilibrium level of real income and real rates in the economy has also been demonstrated. However, the stagflation of the late 1970s brought the Keynesian model into question and resulted in the rise of Friedman's monetarist alternative. Interestingly, the Hicks-Hansen IS–LM interpretation of Keynes is robust enough to demonstrate the monetarist view that money can only affect real income in the short run, while in the long run, inflation is inherently a monetary phenomenon.

Chapter 3

Stagflation and the Rise of Monetarism

Policy makers' repeated attempts to manipulate the economy in the 1960s and early 1970s, along the lines inferred to be possible under the Keynesian model, produced unexpected results, specifically, stagflation. Ian McLeod coined the term in a speech given to the UK Parliament in 1965 concerning the unfortunate macroeconomic developments England was experiencing at that time. Stagflation is essentially a situation in which the inflation rate remains stubbornly high or rises even as the economy slows and the jobless rate rises. In the United States, stagflation emerged in the mid-1970s when the country underwent five consecutive quarters of negative real GDP, but inflation nearly tripled in 1973 and hit double digits in 1974 and 1975 as the jobless rate climbed to 9 percent in May of that year. Initially, economists blamed the situation on OPEC's oil embargo of 1973, but this adverse dynamic proved to be more persistent than did the associated spike in oil prices.

The quadrupling of crude oil prices to $12 per barrel (the equivalent of $75 today) resulted in a decidedly higher cost for individuals and corporations and was seen as reducing employment while boosting inflation. However, President Nixon's abandoning the gold standard, and his on-again, off-again experiment with wage and price controls, were also blamed for the unexpected behavior of inflation. The sharp decline in the exchange value of the dollar reinforced the accelerating inflation feedback loop. The persistence of unacceptably high inflation and the stickiness of wages in the face of weak labor markets resulted in a push to find a new approach that could explain these developments that the Keynesian model had not anticipated.

Empirical studies began to reveal a significant weakness in the Keynesian model as far back as the second half of the 1960s, when fiscal stabilization policies, designed to curb inflation, failed to work their expected magic. In light of this failure, some economists began to suggest that the inflation problem was a result of the rapid growth in money late in the decade. The resulting debate led economists to question which policy lever was more important: fiscal or monetary policy? The results were unexpected, as it became statistically evident that monetary, not fiscal, policy was more important in many ways. The policy-lever debate heated up after Leonall Andersen and Jerry Jordan, two researchers from the Federal Reserve Bank of St. Louis, published a study in which they concluded that monetary policy was significantly more influential in determining growth in the economy than was fiscal policy. The Andersen-Jordan model ratcheted up the intensity of the macro policy debate and helped set the stage for the rise of monetarism.

Before we get into the quantity theory of money and revolution in monetary policy under Fed Chairman Volcker, a review of the Keynesian aggregate demand and supply model will allow a better understanding of the fundamental differences between these competing views of how the economy works.

Aggregate Demand and Supply in the Keynes Model

The aggregate demand curve can be generated directly from the interaction of the IS–LM analysis by varying the price level, which subsequently shifts the position of the LM curve relative to the IS curve. This results in a different pair of income and interest rates that satisfies both the product market and the liquidity market simultaneously for a given level of money supply being provided to the economy by the Fed:

IS: $Y = C(Y - Y(Y)) + I(R) + G$ and LM: $M/P = L(Y, R)$ where M is given.

Remember that in the Keynesian model, money is very narrowly defined as the sum of currency in circulation and checkable deposits. This allows for tight control on the money supply by the Fed, justifying the assumption that this key variable can be treated as exogenous in the model. Even in the Keynesian model, money plays a crucial role in the economy but is not the policy tool of choice.

Aggregate supply is generally modeled in the Keynesian world by employing the Phillips curve in conjunction with a production function. Together, they deliver a unique level of output for the labor provided, given a level of productive resources available in the economy. In the short term, assuming a fixed level of productive resources in an economy is realistic, given that it takes time for investment spending to alter the level of capital stock.

The inverse relationship between wage/prices and the jobless rate implied by the Phillips curve ensures an upward-sloping aggregate supply curve. As companies seek to increase employment, they mark up wages, which increases the degree of utilization in the labor market. This then increases output through the production function and establishes an upward-sloping aggregate supply curve. The point where a downward-sloping aggregate demand curve intersects an upward-sloping aggregate supply curve determines the equilibrium level of output and prices in the economy consistent with equilibrium in the product, liquidity, and labor markets.

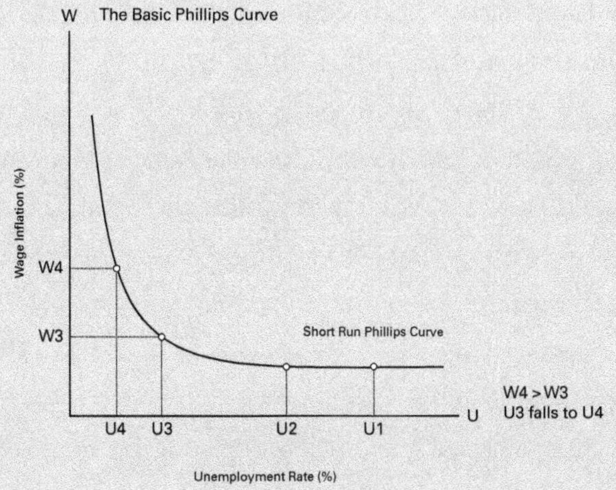

fig 3.1

Phillips Curve or Consumer Price Index (CPI) vs. Inflation

In a world of fully fixable wages and prices, the Phillips curve determines the trade-off between the degree of slack in the labor market and the associated wage rate demanded by workers and paid by firms. A stable trade-off between the jobless rate and wages was generally assumed by economists but was eventually documented statistically by W. H. Phillips in 1958. Phillips studied the relationship between wage inflation and the unemployment rate in the United Kingdom between 1861 and 1957. Specifically, his work found a consistent inverse relationship: When unemployment was high, wages increased slowly; when unemployment was low, wages rose rapidly. Phillips saw this empirical relationship as supporting the notion that the tighter the labor market, the faster firms had to raise wages to attract workers, given the relatively fixed supply of labor in the short run.

Economists quickly emulated Phillips's analysis in other countries, and the close fit discovered in the data led economists like Paul Samuelson and Robert Solow to build the Phillips curve relationship into their large-scale econometric model. These structural models were then simulated to show how fiscal policy could be manipulated to counter the business cycle. Figure 3.1 shows a generalized version of the Phillips curve where a decline in the jobless rate from U3 to U4 boosts the wage rate in the economy from W3 to W4.

The perceived stability of this relationship implied a menu of different options available for policy makers to exploit. As computers increased the availability of data and shortened the time needed to run simulations of difference equilibrium based on policy, alternative economic scenarios could be estimated statistically. This empirical work tempted policy makers to try to fine-tune the economy in an effort to end the business cycle.

The Kennedy tax cut implemented under Lyndon Johnson and Nixon's 1971 budget demonstrated that Capitol Hill completely embraced the Keynesian model. Unfortunately, the Phillips curve proved to be less stable than expected, and the results predicted by these large-scale econometric models failed to materialize. In fact, economists like Milton Friedman and Edmund Phelps began to question the theoretical underpinnings of the trade-off between joblessness and wages even as the Keynesian model was dominating policy discussions. They argued that well-informed, rational employers and workers would pay attention to real wages, not nominal wages. In their view, real wages would adjust to make the supply of labor equal to the demand for labor; and the unemployment rate would remain at the level associated with the real wage rate, which they called the natural rate of unemployment. Essentially, any attempt to exploit the Phillips curve and push the jobless rate below the natural rate would, in Phelps's view, result in rising inflation expectations. This, then, would result in the Phillips curve shifting to the left, tracing out a vertical long-run relationship between wages and the unemployment rate. Even if the Phillips curve could be exploited for a time, expectations would eventually adjust, retuning the labor market to its natural rate of unemployment. Both Friedman and Phelps argued that the government could not permanently trade higher inflation for a lower jobless rate, and the stagflation that developed in the late 1970s–early 1980s proved their case.

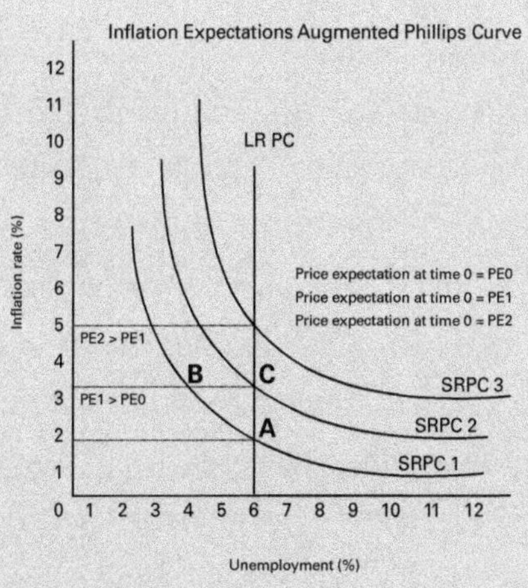

fig 3.2

Alternative Models

Stagflation brought into question the fundamental conclusions of the Keynesian IS–LM aggregate demand/aggregate supply model. The principal component brought into question was the Phillips curve, which accounted for the upward-sloping aggregate supply curve in the Keynesian model. This supposed trade-off between wages, prices, and the unemployment rate was assumed to be exploitable, and provided the logic behind Keynesian-inspired stabilization policies. Stubborn upward pressure on prices despite increasing slack in the economy in the late 1960s and 1970s, however, led to increased interest in an alternative approach being championed by Milton Friedman and other like-minded economists generally referred to as the Chicago school. Their work was built on the quantity theory of money and was generally empirical in nature. The key result of their statistical approach was the belief that inflation was inherently a monetary phenomenon. Their work strongly suggested that stagflation was the result of the Federal Reserve mismanaging monetary policy by following the Keynesian approach of supporting fiscal policy decisions.

By targeting interest rates and relying on fiscal policy to fine-tune the business cycle, the monetarists asserted that the Fed had let excessive money growth lead to an inflation psychology. This embedded inflation psychology manifested itself in a wage-price spiral. The monetarists' prescription of targeting money growth instead of interest rates eventually replaced the Keynesian doctrine. But its dominance proved to be short-lived, as financial innovation quickly rendered a key tenet of their model—the stability of the velocity of money—obsolete. The result would be the development of a new form of Keynesian analysis, this time built on the micro foundations of macroeconomics.

Before discussing the Friedman-Schwartz monetarist model and the New Keynesian school, which have come into vogue in the past thirty years, we need to recognize that money played a key, but passive, role even in the Keynesian model.

Chapter 4

Friedman and Schwartz

Although the Keynesian model failed to live up to its promises, the model framework created can be utilized to discuss the monetarist approach that replaces Keynes. Where Keynes emphasized the role of the government's tax and spending policies to fine-tune the economy, the monetarists emphasized the role of money supply and the Federal Reserve (Fed) in determining real GDP and inflation. Essentially, Keynes emphasized manipulating the IS curve to shift the aggregate demand curve, while the monetarists (led by Friedman) emphasized the role of money in the economy. Keynes saw the Great Depression as having been caused by insufficient aggregate demand; Friedman viewed the Depression as having been caused by the Federal Reserve and its failure to offset forces in the economy that were reducing liquidity.

The monetarist approach suggests that the economy cannot be fine-tuned; but instead, policy makers should establish a target path for money growth that is consistent with long-term sustainable growth, and then they should adhere to this long-term path. By targeting a rate of money growth consistent with the rate of noninflationary growth, the economy will, over time, achieve its optimal level of growth and employment. Monetarism gained prominence in economic thinking in the late 1970s; by 1979, it was finally adopted by the Federal Reserve in the wake of inflation peaking at 20 percent that year.

Monetarism at Its Most Basic

The quantity theory of money goes back to classical economists like David Ricardo in the early 1800s. The quantity theory in its simplest form is characterized as the close relationship between money stock and price level. Classical economists concentrated on the long-run aspects of the quantity theory, in which changes in money result in changes in nominal magnitudes like the aggregate price level but have no influence on real magnitudes like output or employment. The modern quantity theory postulates that in the short run, changes in the rate of growth in money are followed (with a moderate lag) by changes in total spending, while changes in real variables like output are quickly reversed. Changes in the price level, however, follow changes in liquidity with a slightly longer lag.

The quantity theory is derived from the accounting identity:

$$MV = PQ$$

In other words, money times the velocity of money is exactly equal to nominal output. Velocity is the rate of turnover of money, or how many times a given stock of money changes hands to deliver a specific level of nominal GDP. This equation is often written in a slightly different form, using growth rates instead of levels:

$$m + v = p + q$$

In this form, the rate of growth of money plus the growth of velocity is equal to the inflation rate plus the rate of growth of real GDP.

As an accounting identity, this equation is uncontroversial. What is controversial is the assumption made about the velocity of money. Monetarists view velocity as generally stable, which implies nominal income is largely a function of money supply and/or money growth. The modern quantity theory, or monetarist view, has several key tenets that were found in the late 1970s and 1980s to be consistent with reduced-form models of the economy pioneered by two economists from the St. Louis Federal Reserve, which came to be known as the Andersen-Jordan model. The basic tenets of the model were as follows:

1. Long-run money neutrality or an increase in money would be followed by an increase in the price level with no effect on real activity.
2. Short-run money nonneutrality, or an increase in the money stock, would temporarily alter the course for real measures

of employment and/or output because wages and prices are sticky in the short run.

3. The constant money growth rule: The Fed should target a rate of growth in the money supply that matches that of the real economy. In other words, the Fed should be bound by fixed rules in allowing money supply growth.
4. Interest rate flexibility: The fixed rate of money supply rule was designed to allow maximum flexibility in interest rates.

The classical form of the quantity theory is essentially the Keynesian IS–LM aggregate demand/aggregate supply model, where the aggregate supply curve is vertical in the long run. As such, the monetarist assertion is that fiscal/aggregate demand policies, in the absence of accommodative monetary actions, have little net effect on output and the price level in the short run. Government spending, whether financed by taxes or borrowing from the public, simply results in crowding out private expenditures with little, if any, net increase in output.

A change in the money stock, on the other hand, exerts a strong, independent influence on total spending. Monetarists conclude that actions by the Federal Reserve that result in changes in the money stock should be the main tool of economic stabilization. Essentially, the increases and/or decreases in money stock shift the LM curve to right/left, altering the level of output and prices in the short run, but only prices in the long run as the inflation-adjusted Phillips curve shifts laterally upward. This shifts the LM back leftward to its original output level. In other words, money illusion may exist in the short run, but inflation expectations quickly react and the LM curve shifts back to its original position.

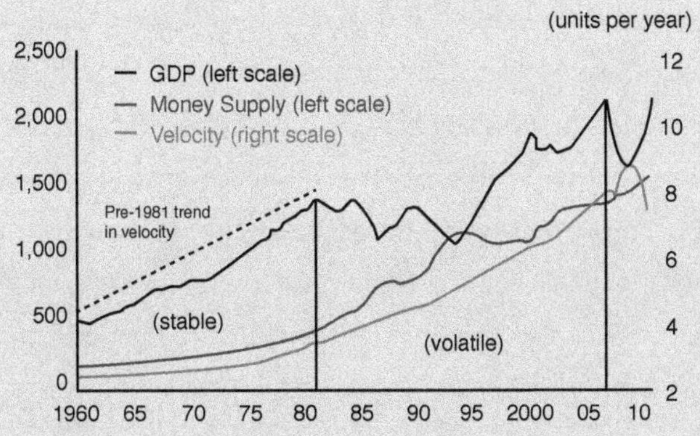

fig 4.1

Source: Board of Governors, US Federal Reserve System

Velocity of Money

Working through the quantity theory of money, the monetarists' model begins with the assumption that the rate of turnover of money is fixed by the banking system's internal rigidities, and that the existing pool of capital and labor is fixed, as is the level of real output. As such, a change in the rate of growth of money tends to be reflected in changes in the price level. This view of the economy explains why the monetarists suggest aggregate stabilization policies should focus on maintaining a steady, long-run, noninflationary rate of money growth consistent with the economy's underlying ability to grow and the target rate of inflation acceptable to the public.

This conclusion tended to be borne out of the empirical analysis done at that time (see "Velocity of Money" graph).

More important, the reduced-form models being studied in places like the University of Chicago, Columbia University, and institutions like the St. Louis Federal Reserve found solid statistical support for the monetarist view. Andersen-Jordan–type models found that changes in federal expenditures—that is, fiscal policy—had a positive influence on real growth for only a few quarters before the effect began to turn strongly negative and quickly net to zero after just five quarters. Meanwhile, these models also found that changes in money growth had only a temporary effect on real variables like employment and output, but after a longer period (sixteen quarters), the effect was almost completely, or 96 percent, reflected in prices.

Ready for Prime Time

A combination of accumulating empirical evidence supporting the monetarist view and the growing political crisis surrounding stagflation resulted in the ascendance of the monetarist school over the Keynesian model. Federal Reserve Chairman Volcker brought monetarism out of the shadows of academia and into the light in late 1979. After returning home from an IMF meeting in Belgrade on October 2, 1979, the newly appointed Fed chief called a special Federal Open Market Committee (FOMC) meeting just four days later, or ten days before the regularly scheduled meeting. The inflation pressures building in the United States and the associated rapidly declining value of the dollar created a sense of emergency among policy makers and politicians that something needed to be done fast. Average inflation had rocketed to 10.6 percent in the first eight months of 1979, from 7.6 percent in 1978. In September 1979, inflation soared to a high of 11.9 percent over the previous year, and the other central bankers present at the IMF meeting pressed Volcker to take bold action.

On October 6, 1979, he presented the FOMC with two possible means of attacking inflation. The traditional path would be to follow the Keynesian model and significantly increase the effective Fed funds rate target, for which the committee would bear the political cost. Alternatively, they could adopt a radical new money supply targeting approach and allow markets to set the level of short-term interest rates. Essentially, the Fed had only two policy options: (1) it could either target the funds rate or allow money growth to match the demand for money in the economy; or (2) it could fix money growth and let interest rates adjust the demand for money to the supply being targeted by the Fed.

The cleverness of this plan, apart from the huge publicity it created, was that it took the Fed out of the role of determining the Fed funds rate, which is a highly political decision. Fed insiders suggested that what convinced the committee to go along with adopting the new operating procedure was Fed governor David Lindsey's observation that the Fed would never select the right level for the funds rate on its own because the volatility it implied would be more than the committee could deal with on its own.

Policy makers hoped this dramatic shift would send the markets a strong signal of its resolve to fight inflation and its intention to return the economy to more stable times after years of failed, start-stop policy changes. Now that monetarism was being put into practice, would the Fed be able to stay the course?

The first test came within weeks of the policy shift. Between December 1979 and February 1980, the 10-year Treasury spiked to 12 percent from 10.5 percent as headline CPI (Consumer Price Index) soared to 14.2 percent year-over-year. At the same time, evidence began to surface that the economy was faltering under the weight of higher rates. The Fed funds rate had climbed to 19 percent by March 1980. Making matters worse, the credit control authorized by President Carter at the end of 1979 quickly plunged the economy into a deep recession. To counter the drag, the Fed was forced to cut the Fed funds rate to 9 percent by July 1980 to turn the economy around. Following the failed experiment with credit control, the Fed's quick action brought the economy roaring back. By the fall of 1980, the Fed funds rate was back to 13.25 percent and the 10-year was back to 10.5 percent, suggesting that the new operating procedure had broken the back of the inflation psychology that had gripped the economy. As energy prices climbed, the Fed funds rate rose to 20 percent by December. The chairman defended the Fed's policy stance as the least-cost alternative to allow inflation to remain embedded in the system relative to the cost of the emerging recession. Staying the course worked, the recession ended, and 1981–1982 inflation was back down around 4 percent.

What's Old Is New

The Fed's experiment with monetarism ended in October 1993, when the FOMC returned to actively targeting the Fed funds rate, but now with enhanced credibility behind its inflation stabilization policies. The principal reason behind the movement away from money supply targeting was the clear breakdown in the relationship between velocity and the economy. The rapid rise in short-term interest rates and the push by financial institutions to compete with new, nonbank financial products like money market mutual funds led to the development of interest-bearing checking accounts and sweep accounts that rapidly blurred the line between savings and transaction balances. The Fed tried to adjust for these financial innovations by altering the definition of the monetary aggregates, but none of these adjustments proved effective. Instead, it became clear that the line between transactions and savings balances became permanently blurred—weakening the statistical argument for the Fed's targeting money supply. Instead, in the post-1982 world, the Fed had maintained its credibility by emphasizing its role in controlling inflation as the means through which it could satisfy its dual mandates. More to the point, the role of monetary policy is to ensure the inflation genie never gets out of the bottle again.

Monetary Aggregates and Components	MB	M1-A	M1-B	M2	M3
Notes and coins in circulation (outside Federal Reserve Banks and the vaults of depository institutions) (currency)	✓	✓	✓	✓	✓
Notes and coins in bank vaults (vault cash)					
Federal Reserve Bank credit (required reserves and excess reserves not physically present in banks)					
Traveler's checks of non-bank issuers		✓	✓	✓	✓
Demand deposits (non interest bearing)		✓	✓	✓	✓
Other checkable deposits (OCDs), which consist primarily of negotiable order of withdrawal (NOW) accounts at depository institutions, credit union share draft accounts, ATS accounts on automatic transfer to checking accounts and demand deposits at nonbank financial institutions			✓	✓	✓
Savings deposits				✓	✓
Time deposits less than $100,000 and money-market deposit accounts for individuals				✓	✓
Large time deposits, institutional money market funds, short-term repurchase and other larger liquid assets					✓
All money market funds					

MB: is referred to as the monetary base or total currency. This is the base from which other forms of money (like checking deposits, listed below) are created and is traditionally the most liquid measure of the money supply.

M1-A, M1-B: Bank reserves are not included in M1.

M2: Represents M1 and "close substitutes" for M1. M2 is a broader classification of money than M1. M2 is a key economic indicator used to forecast inflation.

M3: M2 plus large and long-term deposits. Since 2006, M3 is no longer published by the US central bank. However, there are still estimates produced by various private institutions.

***fig* 4.2**

Source: Board of Governors, US Federal Reserve System

Definition of Monetary Aggregates: M1-A, M1-B, M2, M3

Chapter 5

A New Keynesian Alternative

Financial innovation rendered the monetarist model obsolete just as stagflation revealed the weakness in the Keynesian model. Both theories rested on the assumption that there were some key stable relationships in the economy that could be exploited by policy makers. The Keynesian model assumed an exploitable Phillips curve trade-off between nominal wages and the degree of slack in the labor market. The unexpected rise of inflation expectations in the real world, as a result of policy makers trying to tame the business cycle, resulted in a vertical aggregate supply curve and discredited the Keynesian model. The monetarist approach replaced the Keynesian approach—and the monetarist reduced-form empirical approach that was adopted by the Federal Reserve in late 1979 in reaction to stagflation also rested on an assumption that proved incorrect.

Milton Friedman's view of the world claimed that rational consumers would realize the inflationary implications of Keynesian fiscal policy and would adjust their labor supply to maintain their real wages. This implied that inflation was a monetary phenomenon and that the central bank would be best served by targeting a rate of growth of money supply consistent with that of the economy's long-term underlying ability to grow. Here again, the quantity theory only worked in practice if the rate of turnover of money—its velocity—was stable over time.

When the Fed adopted a monetarist approach in October 1979, interest rates spiked, and the increased volatility of short-term rates triggered new forms of bank and nonbank liabilities designed to protect consumers from rate volatility. These new hybrid forms of deposits altered the relationship between money and the economy by blurring the lines between savings and transaction balances. The increased volatility in the velocity of money left the monetarists in the same position as the Keynesians—with a model where the critical assumption proved to be invalid. Economists, as a result, were again looking for a new approach, and New Keynesianism was born. This approach placed greater emphasis on the micro foundations of macroeconomics, and looked to preserve the best aspects of classical Keynesian. A crucial component of the New Keynesian school of thought was the role of wage and price rigidities to explain the persistence of unemployment and macroeconomic disequilibrium.

Key elements of this new approach include the following.

1. Many markets are imperfectly competitive (i.e., they have a degree of monopoly power). Therefore, firms having the ability to set prices may be reluctant to cut prices in the face of a decrease in demand, leading to price rigidity.

2. Labor markets are also imperfect; wages tend to be sticky, especially to the downside. Unions and firms both tend to be resistant to nominal wage cuts.
3. Shocks to the economy, such as a temporary drop in demand, tend to result in higher real wages and increased unemployment.
4. Real interest rates may depart from natural interest rates, so it is the Federal Reserve's responsibility to restore the correct interest rate to avoid macro instability.
5. Both monetary and fiscal policy play a role in stabilizing the economy, but monetary policy is the preferred tool, due to reduced lags.

These new elements require a micro approach rather than a macro one in order to build these changes into the model. Because the Keynesian aggregate demand model is well grounded in the micro world, the key changes of the New Keynesian model are supply side—in particular, modeling the demand and supply of labor.

To better understand the New Keynesian approach, the micro foundations of labor demand and supply are outlined below in very simple terms. The model depicted can be easily modified to build in the wage and price rigidities evident in the real world, closing the circle for the role money plays in macroeconomic theory.

Micro Foundations of Labor Demand and Supply

Aggregate supply can be modeled by looking at the interaction between the demand and supply for labor—in conjunction with a production function that delivers a unique level of output for the labor provided, and a given level of productive resources in the economy. In the short run, a fixed level of production resources is a realistic assumption, given that it takes time for investment spending to alter the level of capital stock. By altering the level of wages, the level of labor provided is either increased or decreased, and through the production function the level of output is altered. Using a simple markup model, from wages to prices, shifts the aggregate supply model into the same price, output space of the aggregate demand curve and the Keynesian aggregate demand/aggregate supply model is now complete.

The micro foundation of the aggregate supply curve is determined by the demand and supply for labor. The demand side of the labor market comes directly from the theory of the firm—in that profit-maximizing companies are seen adding labor input to their production function until the point that the marginal increase in revenue from adding the next worker is exactly equal to the marginal cost of employing the next worker. Specifically, the firm will continue to hire workers until the change in revenue is equal to the change in cost for the firm. In other words, firms will continue to hire until the next worker added is paid the value of their marginal output. This yields a downward-sloping labor demand curve, which traces the combination of wages and labor inputs that a profit-maximizing firm will demand. Aggregate demand for labor can then be found by adding up the labor demanded by all firms in the economy at each specific wage rate.

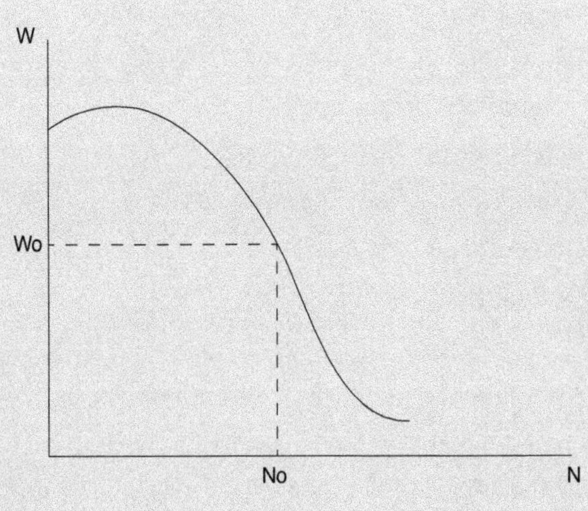

fig 5.1

Aggregate Demand for Labor Curve

The micro foundations of labor supply are subsequently modeled by studying the indifference curve and budget constraints that an individual will face in choosing between work and leisure time, given the finite time available in any given day, week, or month. Specifically, the average worker wants to achieve the mix of income and leisure that is expected to be most satisfying. In other words, the worker wants to maximize the utility he or she receives from their income and their leisure time, subject to the constraint that their expected income is equal to their real wage multiplied by the hours worked. The more leisure time consumed, the less they earn where their utility is positively related to both income and leisure time:

$$U = U\,(Y/P,\, S)$$

U = **utility**
Y = **nominal income**
S = **leisure time**
P = **prices**
Subject to: $y = W/P(T - S)$
T = **total hours available**

Graphically, the indifference curves implied by the utility function U are assumed to be convex to the origin. This suggests there is a trade-off for the worker between how much they earn and their personal time. As such, each indifference curve represents the various pairs of income and leisure that yield the same level of satisfaction or utility to the consumer. Each successively higher indifference curve yields a higher level of utility or satisfaction to the worker. The worker optimizes his or her preference by supplying the amount of labor that places him or her on the highest indifference curve, given the constraint imposed on maximum income and/or leisure time consumed. By changing the wage rate paid by firms, the individual's budget constraint rotates to the right, and the average worker can attain successively higher utility curves. This generally results in less leisure time being consumed or more hours worked.

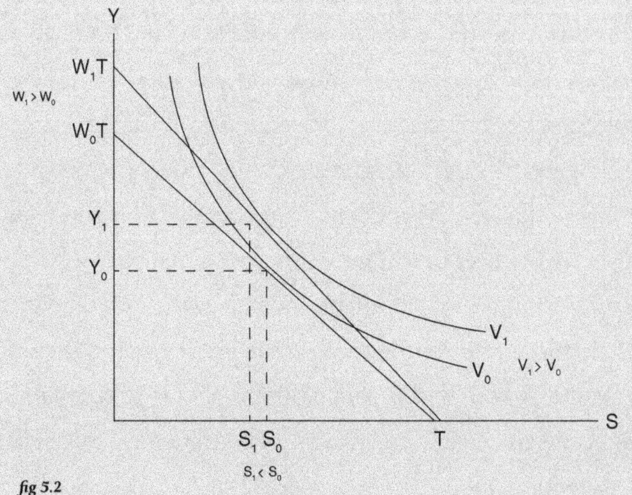

fig 5.2

Workers' Indifference Curves, Budget Constraint, and Labor Supply Curve

Repeating this process over and over at successively higher wage rates traces out an upward-sloping labor supply curve for an average worker. Horizontally adding up the hours worked at each wage rate across the pool of available workers results in an upward-sloping aggregate labor supply curve. Joining the aggregate supply curve for labor with the aggregate demand curve for labor imputed form profit maximizing firms and establishes the equilibrium level of employment and wage rate paid at a given level of prices in the economy.

By subsequently increasing or decreasing the exogenous price level embedded in the labor market model described above, the equilibrium level of labor demanded and supplied in the economy is either increased or decreased in accordance with the elasticity of the aggregate demand and supply curves for labor. The resulting labor input is then converted into output by the economy's production function, given a fixed level of capital stock, and traces out an upward-sloping aggregate supply curve for the economy. The intersection of the downward-sloping aggregate demand curve generated by the Keynesian IS–LM model and the aggregate supply curve consistent with equilibrium in the labor market determines the equilibrium price level and income in the broad economy and develops the jumping-off point for the New Keynesian alternative, which has been in place for almost thirty years and now seems to be running into its own limitations. Specifically, the exceptionally low level of interest rates experienced since the 2007–2008 financial crises and the economy's limited response to the lowest rates in decades suggest a Keynesian liquidity trap may have resurfaced.

Summary

The evolution of macroeconomic thinking since the Great Depression can be divided into three major periods: (1) the Keynesian period; (2) the monetarist period; and (3) the New Keynesian period. Money plays a unique role in each of these views of how the economy functions and, as a result, so does monetary policy. However, instead of focusing on the Fed, as most studies tend to do, the remainder of this book will review money: its role in the economy; the different forms it has taken; the different monetary systems that have been employed domestically; the role of the reserve currency; and how currency valuations are determined, at least in theory. The intent is to fill in the missing pieces in a literature rich in analyses of the Fed and its role in controlling money, interest rates, and the economy, but which is limited in analyzing a primary target of Fed policy and macro modeling.

We will look, in detail, at the different forms money has taken throughout history and, more important, the types of money used in this country through its relatively short history. Additionally, we look at the different monetary regimes that have been implemented and why they all failed. This analysis will bring us from wampum to today's fiat currency model. The costs and benefits associated with each of the different currency regimes experimented with over the decades will also be addressed in the next section.

We will then look at the more recent economic/monetary developments and how, despite a fully flexible fiat currency model, the risk of deflation is again threatening the economy. Deflation exacerbated the economic contraction of the 1930s. Keynes explained the failure of the classical school of economics and credited the insufficient liquidity provided to the economy by the central bank as a key contributor to the Depression. In contrast, global excess supply appears to be the culprit behind today's deflation concerns, suggesting that economic policy may again be at a crossroads, requiring the adoption of new policy tools or at least a new, more coordinated use of fiscal and monetary policy to avoid a repeat of past mistakes.

Section 2

The Practical Side to Money in the Economy

Chapter 6

What Is Money?

In Section 1, we explored the central role money plays in the post-Depression world. We traced the Keynesian macro model and the policy prescription implied to avoid another such period of economic dislocation. Money plays a more passive role in the Keynesian world, even though its ability to expand aggregate demand was evident in the mathematical framework Hicks and Hansen provided for the post-Depression interpretation of how the economy works. Monetary policy was expected to simply support the fiscal policy decisions undertaken at the time. Essentially, the Fed was to expand money supply in order to keep real balances steady—even as prices drifted higher—or, in other words, target an unchanged level of short-term interest rates as a means of increasing consumer and corporate confidence.

The stagflation that surfaced in response to policy makers' repeated attempts to exploit the Phillips curve in the Keynesian world led to a breakdown in business and consumer confidence, political uncertainty, and a sharp decline in the exchange value of the dollar. The backlash to stagflation, both domestically and internationally, created a sense of urgency and prompted the adoption of a new macroeconomic approach by the Federal Reserve under Paul Volcker in late 1979.

The empirical work done by economists at the St. Louis Federal Reserve Bank and the theoretical work of Friedman and Schwartz elevated the quantity theory to the point where it replaced Keynes and put money growth and therefore the Fed at the center of macroeconomic thinking. Although Chairman Volcker's shift to monetarism is credited with breaking the back of inflation expectations and ending the wage-price spiral at the heart of stagflation, it fell out of favor fairly quickly, and by the early 1990s it was replaced with a hybrid model called Neo- (New) Keynesianism. This approach, arguably still in vogue today, sees money as an important determinant of nominal growth but also recognizes that the Phillips curve is not stationary.

Because money is such a critical determinant of economic growth, it is essential to understand what money is, what forms it has taken, and why currency regimes have tended to fail throughout history if we are to understand the deflation risks currently confronting economies around the world and why the Fed and markets are closely monitoring the recent evolution of monetary dynamics. Our analysis will touch on alternative approaches to policy currently being discussed, like Modern Monetary Theory (MMT). We will also discuss the recent introduction of Bitcoin and other cryptocurrencies, and we will look at the reason behind the development of these currency alternatives. Although this could be viewed as evidence that the dollar's role as the primary reserve currency is under attack, we will see that these alternatives suffer from the same drawbacks as commodity-based currencies and are therefore unlikely to pose a serious threat to the dollar's central role in global trade.

Origins of Money

To understand the evolution of money, we must recognize that the primary motivation behind its development was to simplify transactions between individuals. Anthropologists believe that money, along with language, allowed early people to solve problems through cooperation. In particular, trade led to rising living standards, and money also facilitated intergenerational wealth transfers. As such, there are three basic theories behind the origins and creation of money: trading, social, and religious purposes.

Most economists subscribe to transaction's role in the creation of money. This view suggests that money is a valuable commodity in and of itself, much like the value attached to agricultural products, rare shells, wampum, or other so-called collectibles, including gold and silver. Unfortunately, the transition beyond simple agricultural commodities as a means of exchange requires an understanding of implied contracts and a legal system to enforce them. It also requires recognition of private property. Although these institutions were evident in the more advanced societies in Western Europe, that was not the case back in the hunter-gatherer days—yet collectibles were still being used as a form of money from very early times.

The second theory behind the origin of money is that it was created for social purposes—for such things as arranging marriages to reparations for casualties of war. This is a plausible reason for creating money, but it is not complete enough to be used as a persuasive argument as to why it was developed.

The third theory suggests that money was created for religious purposes. It has been suggested that it was first developed in Eastern temples as a prescribed sacrifice to the gods and payment to priests for their services. Historians find support for this theory in the vast amounts of gold and silver that Alexander the Great is rumored to have discovered in Eastern Asia as far back as 330 BCE. In fact, historical records suggest that between 1500 BCE and 1000 BCE, the medium of exchange appears to have shifted from cattle to gold by weight. It appears that temples, which were the center of communities, probably played a key role in transforming gold into money. Why gold? It was the easiest metal for ancient people to mine from rocks in riverbeds. Copper was the next easiest, while silver required more advanced techniques to identify and process. Note that this view stands in contrast to gold's rarity for determining its use as money. Under this alternate theory, the value of gold was probably originally set by priests instead of being determined by the cost of mining and shaping it into a physical coin.

Historians and anthropologists believe that tribes of hunter-gatherers used collectible objects as a form of money even before large-scale trade networks were developed. These early forms of money improved the workings of small societal groups by eliminating the need for simultaneous coincidence of need that underlies a barter economy. Collectibles were first used as money because these objects were desired in their own right. The early Clovis people, some 12,000 years ago, used long chert blades that served only for ornamental purposes as a form of money. Others used furs, animal teeth, or necklaces made of snail shells as a means of exchange. Moreover, archaeologists have found strands of shells dating back some 75,000 years in African caves that they believe were used as a medium of exchange and a unit of account.

More recently, American Indians used strands made of specific clamshells, or wampum, as money. These strands could be added together or split into smaller pieces, increasing their versatility as money. Eventually, the British colonists living in the New World adopted wampum as a local currency because the UK trading companies tried to control the flow of goods within the colonies by limiting the supply of gold and silver coins minted in the United Kingdom. This, in fact, is how "clams" entered the American vernacular as another name for money. There are reports that a Dutch governor of New York even took out a large loan from a local bank denominated in wampum instead of coin of the realm.

A key conclusion to be gleaned from these three theories of the origin of money is that any form of money only has value because people working together in supportive social groups and under legal systems agreed to its value. Money has value because it is accepted as a medium of exchange and it is accepted for paying taxes. As such, money is a public resource and is issued for the common good. Because of this aspect, it has been suggested that money should only be issued by the government or central authority of a community and not by private institutions like banks. This is an oversimplification of reality; if banks or any other issuer of money are regulated by the government or a government-sponsored central bank, ensuring that the flow of money is supportive of the community's common goals, then the issuer of a specific form of money is immaterial.

To this point, the Federal Reserve has been in existence since December 1913 to control the monetary system and, by doing so, to hopefully avoid economically disruptive financial panics. More recently, the Fed has been charged with conducting the country's monetary policy to support maximum sustainable employment, stable prices, and moderate long-term interest rates. Monetary policy has been conducted according to this mandate since 1977, and inflation has remained well under control since the late 1980s.

Hard to Define

Money is one of those things that we know as soon as we see it, but that we have difficulty defining; when we try, we quickly realize that there is much more here than appears on the surface. Because money is such a big part of our day-to-day lives, we take its existence for granted and overlook that history is rife with forms of money that have failed. Museums around the world devote entire displays to the various forms money has taken over the ages. These displays generally include stones, shells, tobacco, countless coins, and pieces of paper, along with other objects that lost their acceptability in transactions between individuals. Despite the repeated demise of different forms of currency, several gained enough widespread acceptance to be recognized as payment in international commerce. One of the first of these universally accepted forms of money was the silver drachma, issued by ancient Athens in the fifth century BCE.

What makes something money? And what causes a specific form of money to fall out of favor?

Money has value when all members of a community working under an accepted legal framework accept it as a medium of exchange; and it is accepted by the central authority (governments or religious organizations) as a means of satisfying obligations such as taxes or religious fees. History suggests that in very early communities, religious institutions may have been the primary central authority and held sway over the creation and distribution of money in society. Going forward, however, we will assume that the government is the primary central authority, determining the form of money, its distribution, and management of the currency.

Money's role as the medium of exchange stands out as the principal reason for its existence. The use of money enables enterprises to develop and societies to establish specializations that foster increased growth. However, money also serves as the unit of account and as a store of value. These characteristics are the most often cited by economists.

Instinctively, everyone understands the benefit that an accepted medium of exchange provides to society, but the unit-of-account characteristic of money is often overlooked. Having an accepted unit of account reduces transaction costs between economic agents. It allows for a speedy comparison of the value of different goods in a way that is easy for everyone to understand, which adds additional grease to the wheels of commerce. Money's role as a store of value, on the other hand, gets right to the heart of why all monetary regimes eventually come under pressure. If a particular form of money doesn't hold its value because of inflation, the oversupply of money, or expected inflation (a loss in confidence in the future value of money), then the desire to hold money diminishes and the rush to reduce money balances amplifies the inflation pressure, which eventually drives a particular form of money out of favor. Simply put, people lose confidence in it, and as a result, it declines in value.

Evolution of Money

These community-based currencies initially took the form of commodities that all members of the community valued, such as grain or cattle. Over time, the uncertain supply of these important commodities, due to harvest variabilities, led to the adoption of collectibles as money, with gold, silver, and copper by weight ending up at the top of this stack. As these communities expanded in population and in territory, the power of the central government increased, and it became natural for the central authority to assume control over the origination, distribution, and management of the money in circulation.

Members of the community preferred the money issued by the government over others because it was also used for paying taxes, eventually driving all other forms of money out of existence. Coins minted by the government eventually replaced precious metals by weight as money. A government's minting of coins added additional value to the currency because the government determined its value, which was usually greater than its precious metal content and the cost of striking the coin. The expansion of trade among communities subsequently resulted in different sovereign currencies being used for trading purposes, and the currency with the greatest potential to retain its value rose to universal acceptance (i.e., the reserve currency) in settling transactions with foreign buyers and sellers of goods. Expanding commerce and the growing need for money eventually prompted the printing of paper money, which the government then declared to be legal tender. To reduce the political risk of overproducing and distributing money, most modern governments turned this responsibility over to an independent central bank that is responsible for controlling the rate of inflation, which is a key determinant of a currency's value.

A *reserve currency* is a currency that is held in significant quantities by governments and foreign institutions as part of their foreign exchange reserves. The reserve currency is commonly used in international transactions, international investments, and all other aspects of international trade, not just between the country issuing the reserve currency and its trading partner but in third-party transactions as well. As such, it is often viewed as a "safe-haven" currency. Essentially, the reserve currency is the international medium of exchange, the international unit of account, and the international store of value. As the medium of exchange, the reserve currency is used to settle all international transactions. International transactions are also denominated in the reserve currency, so it is the unit of account, and in times of international uncertainty, the value of the reserve currency appreciates because it is expected to retain its value as the best of all other currency alternatives.

The history of reserve currencies is fairly checkered—the first currency circulated widely outside its borders was the Greek drachma. This was followed in ancient times by the Roman denarius, the Byzantine solidus, and the Arab dinar. In the Middle Ages, the first reserve currency was the Venetian ducato, and in the Renaissance, the Florentine florin was the dominant currency of international trade. In the eighteenth century, the Dutch guilder emerged as the reserve currency. The unprecedented domination of trade by the Dutch East India Company elevated the guilder to its reserve currency status. However, the modern concept of a reserve currency emerged in the mid-nineteenth century with the introduction of national central banks and the increasingly integrated global economy. By the 1860s, most industrial countries had followed the United Kingdom and placed their currencies on a gold standard. At this time, the UK was also the primary exporter of manufactured goods and services, and about 60 percent of world trade at the time was denominated in pounds.

British banks were expanding overseas, and London had become the global center for insurance and commodity trading. Foreign borrowers came to London in search of funding for new investments in their home countries. The UK's reintroduction of the gold bullion

> standard in 1925 under the Gold Standard Act was designed to restrain inflation that had not receded after World War I, and the gold standard was eventually adopted by many other countries. The result was deflation and a run on the Bank of England's gold reserves. With the onset of the Great Depression, global trade collapsed, and the pound came under speculative attacks. This subsequently forced the country off the gold standard in 1931, and it continued to float until after World War II, when it was tied to gold and the US dollar—the current reserve currency. Although the dollar remains the reserve currency to date, central banks tend to hold more than one currency in their FX (Foreign Exchange) portfolio. The euro, the yen, and even the Chinese renminbi have come to serve as reserve currencies to a lesser extent.

Banks and Money Creation

The definition of money presented above suggests that currency, in any form, is principally used as a medium of exchange, but it also serves as a unit of account and as a store of value (at least as far as economists are concerned). The efficiency gained by using money in transactions between economic agents is seen as the principal factor driving its creation. Alternatively, academics in other fields have suggested that money may have been created to serve a social good. Religious institutions in early societies may have created money as a way of sustaining their temples and priests through donations and/or other fees assessed on members of the community. This view helps explain why money tends to be issued and regulated by a central authority, suggesting that money is also a social good and should, therefore, not be issued by private entities (i.e., banks); yet, in most advanced economies, banks play a central role in the economy.

We will see in this section that money issued by banks in the early history of this country had a very disappointing record. Even money issued by government-chartered banks had a checkered record until the creation of the Federal Reserve in late 1913 to regulate the creation and distribution of the currency. In fact, there were times in our country's relatively short history that several different forms of currency circulated at the same time. A clear understanding of the banking industry's role in the economy will help us better understand why, in modern society, banks play such a central role in the economy, even if the evolution of money implies that only the central public authority should issue and control the money in circulation.

Banks are unique institutions in the world we live in because they are the only private institutions that can expand the money supply. A fractional reserve requirement system allows banks to grow their deposits by making loans with their excess reserves. This ability comes with strings attached. These include not just the requirement to hold reserves against their deposit liabilities, but also subject to a complex web of regulation, capital charges, and supervisory oversight. Banks are for-profit institutions, and it is this trade-off between earning a return and safeguarding deposits where banks tend to get into trouble. As such, before we move on to discussing the different currencies used in this country, it will be instructive to understand the history of our banking industry in this country.

Evolution of the Domestic Banking Industry

Banks are among the oldest business institutions in American history. This reflects the fact that banks were also very important in Europe at the time the New World was discovered. Banks provided important services to the economy from their beginning. They operated as clearinghouses to expedite payments between individuals, businesses, and banks themselves. They also enabled financial intermediation in the economy through their lending books. Banks make their profits and cover their expenses by charging borrowers more for the loans they originate than their cost of funding (the rate they pay depositors). The intermediation role is a bank's primary profit center and is the riskiest aspect of banking. There is always a risk that the borrower will not pay back their loan with the expected interest payment.

A modern economy could not function without a robust banking industry. It is often taken for granted that such financial institutions (like money) always existed when, in fact, this is far from the truth. Colonial America had no banks, and it wasn't until 1781 that Alexander Hamilton spearheaded the push for Congress to charter the nation's first bank—the Bank of North America, located in Philadelphia. Prior to its charter, merchants, wealthy individuals, and banks in Great Britain provided credit in the colonies. Money consisted of foreign coins and paper money issued by the government in each colony. Three years after the Bank of North America was chartered, Boston merchants founded the Massachusetts Bank, and Hamilton became a founder of the Bank of New York. After Hamilton was appointed the first Secretary of the Treasury, he moved quickly to ensure the country had a modern financial system. He restructured the government's debt into US Treasury securities, which paid interest quarterly. To fund the national debt, he instituted the federal revenue system. Hamilton also defined the US dollar in terms of gold and silver coins, which served as reserves for banks that issued paper currency.

In 1790 Hamilton convinced Congress to deal with the debt created by the Revolutionary War by chartering the First Bank of the United States, which he modeled after the Bank of England. The bank was funded with $10 million in capital, $2 million of which was provided by the government, and secured the government's control over the bank and its operations. Domiciled in Philadelphia, the bank had eight branches, one in each major city. Congress was convinced to charter the bank to help facilitate Hamilton's restructuring of war-related debt; but, because the bank was a public company, it was also able to make corporate and individual loans. The bank's lending activities would spark the growth of state-chartered banks and would also create the controversy that would lead Congress not to renew its charter in 1811.

Following Hamilton's lead, state legislatures began to charter banks, and by 1790 there were thirty such institutions doing business in the growing country. Thereafter, the growth of banks took off, with 100 operating by 1810, between 500 and 600 by the 1830s, and some 1,500 to 1,600 in existence at the start of the Civil War. Besides the growth of banks, active security markets were also established in the early 1790s due to the $63 million in Treasury debt Hamilton had issued in addition to the $10 million in stock issued to capitalize the First Bank of the United States. This helped provide liquid benchmark securities that traded on the Philadelphia and New York Exchanges.

Federal debt began to mount again as a result of the War of 1812, and state-chartered banks that had been issuing their own paper currency also suspended the redemption of these notes for gold or silver. Additionally, the multitude of banknotes issued by state-chartered institutions complicated transactions, since these notes had to be discounted based on the quality of the issuing bank and the distance between institutions involved in transactions. These significant shortfalls of a decentralized state charter system led Congress to charter the Second Bank of the United States in 1816. It was charged with promoting a uniform currency.

The second bank functioned as a clearinghouse for other banknotes; as such, it held large quantities of other banknotes in reserve, which it could use to discipline state-chartered institutions if necessary. Thus, this second bank took on the role of banking system regulator. The Second Bank of the United States was structured like its predecessor but was capitalized with $35 million in equity. Initially, the bank was poorly managed and was almost insolvent within the first two years of operation. Following a change of management, the bank functioned profitably and efficiently. However, the bank ran into opposition from newly elected President Andrew Jackson, who saw the bank as too powerful and prone to possible corruption. He therefore refused to renew its charter in 1836, and the era of "free banking" began.

A rapidly growing country needed more banks, and states responded with "free banking laws," under which banks were now allowed to be established simply by depositing bonds with state auditors, which served as the reserves backing the banknotes they issued. These free banks were also required to redeem their banknotes for gold or silver on demand. Hundreds of new banks were established under these new rules. Without a central regulator, the expanding banking system of the 1830s through 1850s experienced a series of banking crises. These crises tended to be triggered by depositors demanding that banks redeem their notes for gold or silver on demand. If a bank was caught short or was believed to be short on reserves, a run on the bank typically resulted in the failure of the institution and possibly other associated banks. Such crises rocked the system in 1837, 1839–1842, and 1857, leading to multiple bank failures and deep economic downturns with sharply rising unemployment. Rampant counterfeiting of banknotes was another development of the "free banking" period.

The outbreak of the Civil War and the need to finance the war effort led to renewed interest in a national bank. With lessons learned from both the First and Second Banks of the United States, the designers struck out in a new direction. Emulating the "free banking model," a national banking system was established. Specifically, banks could now choose between a national bank charter or a state charter. National banks issued government-printed bills that were backed by federal bonds issued to fund the war effort. To keep state banks from continuing to issue their own paper notes, a new tax was imposed on state banks and such notes ceased to circulate. The national banking system finally established a uniform national currency and lasted from 1863 to 1913, when the Federal Reserve was established in the wake of severe banking panics in 1873, 1893, and 1907. The regularity of these panics and the severe negative effect they had on the economy and joblessness forced Congress to reconsider a centralized national bank.

The Federal Reserve was founded as a decentralized institution in order to avoid concern over the concentration of power that led to the political problems that plagued the first two national banks. As such, the Fed was designed to comprise twelve district banks and a board of governors in Washington, DC. Each district bank operates independently and issues its own money initially backed by the promise to redeem these notes for gold.

The system's role as the government's bank naturally led the Fed to serve as a banker's bank. By taking deposits, making loans, and acting as the primary clearing bank, the Fed also assumed the role of banking regulator. The Fed's role has expanded since its inception in 1913, with most people now seeing the Fed's primary role as establishing the country's monetary policy. However, its more traditional role as bank regulator and lender of last resort remains exceptionally important. With the issuance, distribution, and control of the money supply firmly in the hands of a government-regulated entity, the Federal Reserve System, the evolution of money now satisfies the conditions set out by the anthropologists, sociologists, and historians, in addition to economists. The ability to redeem these Federal Reserve notes for gold, at the time of its establishment, helps explain why individuals ascribe a value to paper money well above its commodity value.

CHRONOLOGY OF BANKING IN THE UNITED STATES

1791–1811	First Bank of the United States
1816–1836	Second Bank of the United States
1837–1863	Free Banking Period
1863–1913	National Banks
1913–	Federal Reserve System

fig 6.1

Source: Macrobond. Mizuho Securities USA, US Department of Treasury

This chapter has covered the origins of money, its definition, the evolution of money, and the banking system's role in creating money. It provides a base from which we can delve into more detailed discussion of the different currency regimes that have been implemented in this country. In particular, we will discuss the gold standard, its mechanics, and the transition to today's fiat monetary system. Specifically, there are two forms of a gold standard: one that uses bullion, and the more modern gold exchange standard that existed in this country until August 1971, when President Nixon closed the gold window and ended the Bretton Woods currency regime. Moreover, we will discuss in detail the US experience with the gold standard and how the retention of a gold exchange standard helped the US dollar become the undisputed postwar reserve currency.

Chapter 7

Money and Gold

Money and gold are often seen as synonymous. Gold coins circulated in ancient times, and even before gold coins were struck, gold (by weight) was used as the principal medium of exchange. Other precious metals have often been used in conjunction with gold, but because gold could be found above the surface, it was easy for even primitive cultures to see its unique qualities. As such, gold has been used by most civilizations as money. Silver, copper, lead, and other precious metals had to be mined and processed before their value could be made evident and, therefore, were used as money much later in history.

The allure of gold as the basis of a currency regime is still evident today, especially in the United States, where a gold exchange/peg standard was maintained until 1971, when President Nixon officially ended gold convertibility. In the past forty-eight years, opponents of today's fiat monetary system have argued for a return to a gold standard to end the debasement of the currency by the government/central bank. Recent advocates of returning to some form of a gold standard included GOP senators Rand Paul and Ted Cruz during the 2016 presidential primaries.

Moreover, the Bitcoin craze of 2017 saw its value surge above $19,700 per coin before the bubble burst. The run-up in Bitcoin reflects a popular desire for incorruptible money that can be used as a store of wealth as well as a medium of exchange and a unit of account. The cryptocurrency craze faded (for now), in part, because of the introduction of a host of other coins like Ethereum, which identified the inherent weakness in a digital currency: Ease of replication can dilute the value of any one cryptocurrency. However, the key factor behind the cryptocurrency movement was the belief that the Fed was moving too slowly to normalize its post–financial market crises accommodation and that inflation was sure to follow. As a result, inflation expectations were on the rise and the dollar was pushed decidedly lower. The limited supply of gold (like the supposed limited supply of Bitcoins) is seen as increasing its value relative to paper—Federal Reserve notes backed by government debt.

Gold's allure as the basis of a currency standard is also evident from the history of banking in the United States (discussed in detail in Chapter 6). Paper money issued by the different banking entities that existed between 1791 and 1913 was generally required to be convertible into gold to enhance its circulation. Even the paper notes issued by the Federal Reserve after its inception in 1913 were made redeemable for gold. Periodically, state legislatures and the US government canceled the ability to redeem paper money for gold prior to

1971, but these were usually during times of war or systemic financial distress to ensure or reestablish financial stability and conserve much-needed gold reserves.

European governments, as well as many others, cut their ties to gold during World War II and never returned. Instead, they adopted a dollar standard under the Bretton Woods agreement. This international currency agreement tied the dollar to gold, while all other participating countries agreed to maintain their exchange rates within a narrow band of the dollar. The Roosevelt administration did the same during the Depression, but the link was reestablished under the Bretton Woods system adopted following the war. We will discuss Bretton Woods in much more detail later, but before we look at international currency regimes, the reader needs to gain a greater understanding of the different types of gold standards and the stormy relationship the United States has had with gold. Chapter 8 will cover the mechanics of a gold standard and the role of monetary policy under the discipline of gold, to round out our discussion of metallic monetary regimes.

Different Forms of a Gold Standard

The gold coin standard was the first regime where the issuance, distribution, and control of the currency was concentrated in the hands of a central authority. The gold coin standard is also called an orthodox gold standard or the traditional gold standard. This form of currency regime was prevalent in many advanced economies (including the United States) up until World War I. Under this form, gold coins circulated in the economy, and other forms of money, such as banknotes or other paper money, were redeemable for gold coin on demand. What makes this the "traditional" form is that coinage was unlimited and free of charge, while there is also free and unlimited melting of gold in the economy. The government stood ready to buy and sell gold at a fixed official price. The free import and export of gold was also allowed. Because gold is universally acceptable, a gold coin standard led to a high level of public confidence in the currency. The relatively fixed supply of gold coins also ensures price stability. The simplicity of a gold coin standard is another important positive; however, several key issues led to its eventual demise as the principal approach to organizing a currency regime. Specifically, people and countries tended to hoard gold during times of crisis, which tends to amplify the problems confronting the economy or society. Deflation was another of the key problems facing countries suffering trade deficits, as gold was transferred to the net exporting countries and the local supply of money contracted. Deflation and the economic contraction associated with a reduction in the money supply became politically unacceptable.

A second type of gold standard employed to correct the imbalances inherent in a gold coin regime was the gold bullion standard. Under this currency model, gold coins did not circulate, but the standard unit of measurement was expressed in terms of a specific quantity of gold and a given purity. Gold coinage was not allowed, and not all paper money or token coins were backed by gold. However, the government guaranteed full convertibility of the currency it issued into gold bullion. This form of currency standard was implemented in many European countries after World War I. Under this standard, the government again stood ready to buy or sell gold at fixed prices, and there was no restriction on the import or export of gold. Because of the unrestricted flow of gold, exchange rate stability was easily maintained. The money supply was also elastic under this regime, since the currency was not fully backed by gold; but convertibility meant a high degree of confidence in the currency, and it was relatively easy to understand. However, in times of trouble, there was still the risk of a run on gold reserves. A run on gold could exceed the government's reserves, causing redemptions to be halted and resulting in confidence issues and/or deflation.

A gold exchange standard was the next regime that was implemented in an attempt to keep the link to gold but avoid its inherent problems in times of economic, political, or military crisis. A gold exchange standard is where the domestic currency is simply denominated in terms of a fixed exchange rate to some other currency that is tied to gold explicitly. No gold coins circulated, and what coins and paper money did circulate could be exchanged only for the currency of the base country. The central bank in this structure holds its reserves in gold and the currency for the base country. Under this form of currency standard, money supply's elasticity and the exchange rate tend to be stable, which helps promote trade. Unfortunately, this system was complex in nature and failed to create the confidence generated when there was gold convertibility. Because the government had the ability to increase money supply but tended to never willingly contract it, there was a tendency toward inflation. Additionally, domestic monetary policy became captive to that of the base country, leading to external insecurity.

The gold reserve standard is the next form. It was experimented with beginning in 1936, when Great Britain, France, and the United States entered into an agreement that allowed for the free flow of gold or foreign currency between the participants to stabilize exchange rates and promote trade. As such, gold was neither a medium of exchange nor a unit of measurement. Therefore, there was no mandate that the domestic currencies were convertible into gold, but there was an exchange stabilization fund established to maintain stable exchange rates. This fund was capitalized with gold and local currencies and its size was kept secret to increase the value of any intervention in the market. This fourth attempt at a gold standard lasted only a few years, until World War II erupted, and in 1939, the conflict rendered it inoperable. However, after the war, a new gold parity standard was established under the terms of the Bretton Woods system of managed exchange rates under the regulation imposed by the International Monetary Fund (IMF). This will be covered in much more detail later in this far-ranging discussion about the role of money in the economy, both in theory and in practice.

GOLD'S ADVANTAGES AND DISADVANTAGES

Before we move on to the ever-evolving nature and attempts by the United States at sustaining a gold standard, it will be instructive to show the advantages and disadvantages of fixing the currency to gold.

Advantages:

1. Price stability is a key virtue of a gold standard. Essentially, a gold standard makes it hard for a government to inflate prices by expanding the money supply (too much money chasing too few goods). Hyperinflation is seen as impossible under a gold standard. However, a sudden expansion in the gold supply can still cause inflation. For example, there was acceleration in prices that followed the California Gold Rush and the dramatic increase in supply it generated.
2. Stability of exchange rates is another advantage of a gold standard. The "spice" flow tends to eliminate imbalances in a country's balance of payments. The gold used to pay for imports reduces the money supply of the importing nation. This generates deflation, which makes exports more competitive and corrects the imbalance.
3. Financial repression (savers earning a return below the rate of inflation) is seen as not being an issue under a gold standard. It can, however, be seen as a transfer of

wealth from creditor to debtor. Also, it is often used by a government to make its debt load easier to pay back by generating inflation.

Disadvantages:

1. A gold standard implies an inequality between countries naturally endowed with a greater supply of the precious metal. China and Russia, for example, are two large producers of gold in the postwar period.
2. It limits growth. Because the supply of gold is essentially fixed at any given point in time, an inelastic money supply limits growth of the economy. As an economy's productive resources grow, so should the money supply. Because a gold standard requires money to be backed by gold, its scarcity limits the economy's ability to grow.
3. Unresponsive monetary policy is another key disadvantage of a gold standard. Because money is fixed to gold, the central bank cannot employ countercyclical monetary policy. The Fed's failure to react to the 1929 stock market crash, and the resulting recession, is often seen as a key reason why the Depression took root and the economy was in consolidation from August 1929 to March 1933—forty-three months of contraction.
4. Official devaluation of the currency under a gold standard tends to be sudden and sharp compared to what could be orchestrated under a fiat currency system.

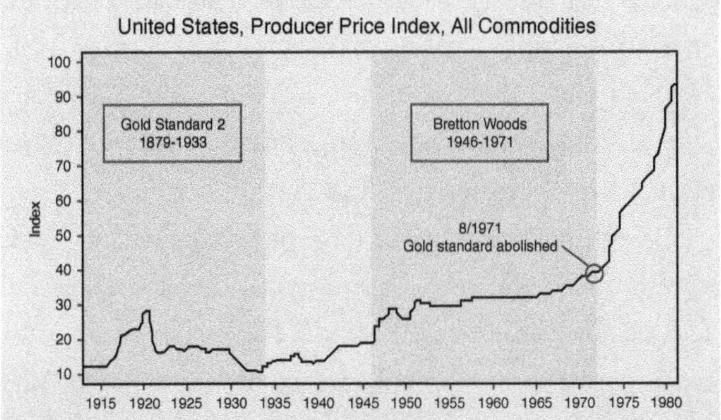

fig 7.1

Source: Macrobond, Mizuho Securities USA, US Bureau of Labor Statistics (BLS)

US PPI Under Gold/Bretton Woods vs. Fiat Money

A Turbulent History with Gold

On again/off again is a fair representation of America's love affair with gold as the medium of exchange, its unit of account, and a store of value. More to the point, the domestic economy has gone through several currency regimes since Hamilton. The Constitution granted Congress "the power to coin money" and to "regulate the value thereof." The Coinage Act of 1792 established the US dollar as the basic monetary unit by providing for free coinage of silver and also providing for the free coinage of gold. As such, the dollar was a bimetallic standard comprising both gold and silver. This act also established a mint ratio where gold was fifteen times more valuable than silver. Gold coins were to satisfy the demand for large denominations, and silver was to form the basis of smaller-denomination coins.

Because coinage was free, if the mint ratio was out of line with the market price for the two metals, then the more valuable metal would be traded away in the open market for the cheaper metal, which would then be sold to the mint. Very early on, this problem with a bimetallic system surfaced. Gold became more expensive in the market than silver, and holders of gold coins sold them for silver, which was then turned into the mint for coinage. The result was that gold coins stopped circulating and the monetary system denigrated into a silver standard. From 1792 to 1834, the United States was principally on a silver standard. To address this problem, Congress reduced the content of gold in the dollar, raising the mint's ratio to 16:1, and the result was a shift from all silver to all gold coins. Additionally, the Appalachian gold discovery played a part in this transition—while the California gold rush (1848–1855) and the Australian finds of 1848 and 1851 were estimated to have quadrupled the supply of gold in the market. This ensured gold's standard dominance until the outbreak of the Civil War.

The rapidly mounting expenses associated with the Civil War prompted both sides to end gold convertibility and resort to issuing paper money. This lasted from 1861 to 1879, even though the war only lasted four years, ending in 1865. In the

South, the suspension of convertibility allowed banks to transfer a substantial portion of their gold reserves to the Confederate Treasury that was paid for with the issuance of paper notes. Although the first such notes were large denominations and not intended to be used as currency, the South quickly began to issue smaller denominations, which formed the basis for their money supply until the surrender at Appomattox rendered these notes worthless. In the North, the cause of the suspension of convertibility was the decision by the Treasury to insist that banks buying some $50 million in Treasury debt do so in gold. This paved the way for the Legal Tender Act in 1862, which authorized the issuance of $150 million in US notes, called greenbacks. This period extended well after the war, even though there was a strong desire to return to gold.

Unfortunately, the prewar mint ratio was so far out of alignment with the market price of gold following the war that a quick return to a gold standard would require a sharp economic adjustment. Not only would the number of greenbacks in circulation need to be reduced substantially, but the resulting deflation would also be devastating. Instead, a more gradual process was adopted that would allow the economy to recover, and the transition back to a peacetime economy was expected to dampen inflation over time. Under this process, the Treasury opted to wait until natural forces slowly brought down the price of gold.

In 1879, the country returned to a metallic standard, but this time gold was the benchmark. Although many people were opposed to a gold-only standard and debated its validity, by 1900 Congress reaffirmed its commitment to gold and relegated silver to small-denominated money. A bimetallic standard of gold and silver should, in theory, be superior to a gold-only standard, according to economists like Milton Friedman. The decision to adopt gold seems to have been motivated by the reality that many European nations had already made the shift, and others were also in the process of converting. Friedman suggests that it was Great Britain's decision to move to just gold that started the transition process in motion globally.

Even though the United States was on a metallic standard since 1792, a variety of banknotes circulated without being legal tender. At different times, paper notes issued by the Treasury also circulated without being legal tender. Much of the money in circulation, under a gold standard, is simply a promise to redeem in gold. To help ensure that paper notes issued by banks were honored, the national banking system (discussed extensively in Chapter 6) was created by the US government in 1863. The instability of the financial system, despite its reliance on gold, led to the creation of the Federal Reserve System in 1913. The new central bank was given the authority to issue Federal Reserve notes that were denominated in gold and were redeemable. As such, the Fed was charged with managing the currency, as well as becoming the primary check-clearing institution and the primary bank regulator. To reduce the risk of a future financial crisis and an associated run on bank deposits (which led to the push for the creation of a central bank), the Fed was given the authority to expand or contract money supply.

World War I prompted President Wilson to suspend the free export of gold when the United States became involved in April 1917. When hostilities ended in November 1918, the suspension was removed. Between 1915 and 1917, when the United States was not involved in the war, the gold standard remained firmly in place.

The Depression era saw another suspension of the gold standard. Despite the Fed's role as bank regulator and lender of last resort, the period from 1930 to 1933 was marked by several bank failures. Economists that studied this dark period blamed the Fed for not providing enough liquidity following the 1929 crash. As a result of the financial crisis, President Roosevelt was forced to suspend convertibility and shift the economy to a hybrid monetary regime.

Through a series of executive orders, legislative actions, and court decisions, the country was taken off the gold standard. All private holdings of gold were nationalized, and a new parity was established at 40 percent below the old rate, which only applied to international transactions, since individuals were not allowed to hold physical gold. The result was a quasi–gold standard. Due to the ongoing national economic emergency, the president was also given legislative authority to authorize the issuance of $3 billion in US notes and compel the Fed to finance up to $3 billion in government borrowing. The government's decision to unilaterally abrogate gold clauses in contracts was held up in the Supreme Court in 1935, allowing the government to meet its debt and interest payments with new-issue, nonconvertible paper money.

Under the Gold Reserve Act of 1934, the dollar was still defined in terms of gold, but gold transactions were limited to official settlements only. This quasi–gold standard continued until after World War II, when a new international monetary regime was established under the Bretton Woods agreement. Bretton Woods (discussed later in this book) firmly cemented the US dollar as the world's reserve currency. In a break with history, the terms of the 1934 act held up through World War II. This break with the more traditional pattern of suspending the gold standard during wars or crises resulted in the transfer of most of the world's gold supply in the United States to pay for armaments provided by domestic manufacturers.

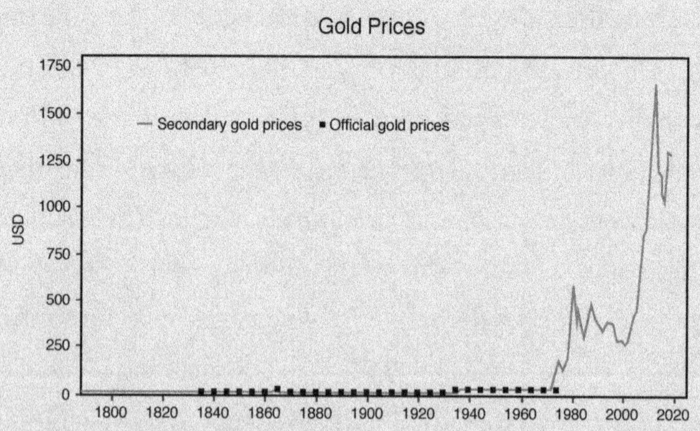

fig **7.2**

Source: Macrobond, Mizuho Securities USA

The Price of Gold Since the Late 1870s

Under the Bretton Woods agreement, the global role of gold was severely limited. Although the US dollar was still denominated in terms of gold, other countries' currencies were defined in terms of gold and the US dollar. Gold could still be used to settle international accounts; however, governments were expected to meet these obligations in currency. The International Monetary Fund (IMF) was established to assist in the exchange process and to provide foreign exchange assistance to countries that were having difficulty maintaining a fixed exchange rate. As a result, a country with an overvalued currency would no longer have to lose gold or experience deflation. IMF credits allowed countries to avoid deflation, but also simply delayed the required adjustment process. This aspect of the new system would become a liability in the late 1960s and 1970s, when inflation gripped the domestic economy because too much money had been issued to keep prices stable or keep gold at its official level.

With the US dollar at the center of the system, inflation exerted significant upward pressure on the price of gold, leading to a drain on US gold holdings. This process reached a tipping point in October 1971. After several international attempts to rebalance the system failed, President Nixon closed the gold window, effectively taking the country off a gold standard. In 1976 the government made it official, no longer denominating the US dollar in terms of gold, and moved explicitly to a fiat monetary system. The net result of this transition was a significant acceleration in the price of gold, reflecting, among other things, a spike in inflation and a surge in debt outstanding. These considerations alone justify including this topic in our wide-ranging discussion on money and why we all should take the risk of the dollar losing its reserve currency status seriously.

The following chapter will discuss the mechanics of a gold standard and the role of monetary policy under the rule of gold. This should increase our understanding of the role money plays in the economy. This analysis will identify what is at stake if policy makers mishandle their privileged position of originating, distributing, and managing money in the economy.

Chapter 8

The Technical Side of a Gold Standard

History shows that the gold standard was no panacea in the United States, though many economic conservatives longed to return to gold, as the discipline it imposes is seen as very desirable. There continues to be much discussion about the benefits that the economy would accrue if it returned to a gold standard. This nostalgic view of the gold standard is not surprising, given (1) the explosion in debt experienced since Nixon broke the gold/dollar link; (2) the inflation experienced during the 1970s and 1980s; and (3) the currency crisis associated with the emergence of stagflation. In fact, the memory of the 1970s wage/price spiral and the damage it inflicted on the economy still haunts domestic policy makers and investors some fifty years later. Moreover, the recent explosion in the Fed's balance sheet, which at its peak monetized more than $3.5 trillion in government debt, has added to this nostalgia and ignited the cryptocurrency craze of 2017–2018.

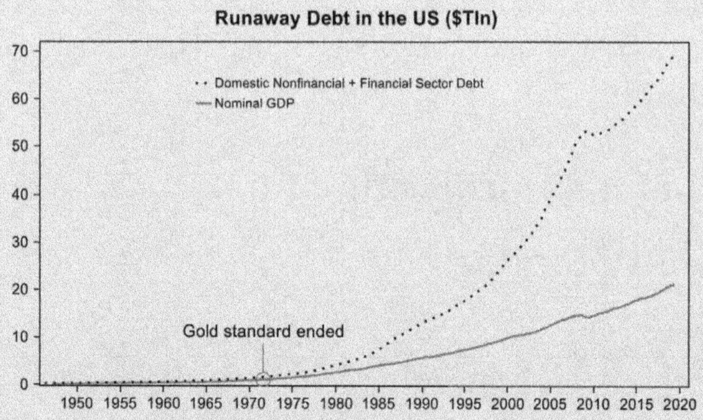

fig 8.1

Source: Macrobond, Mizuho Securities USA, BEA, US Federal Reserve System

US Debt Growth 1940–2020

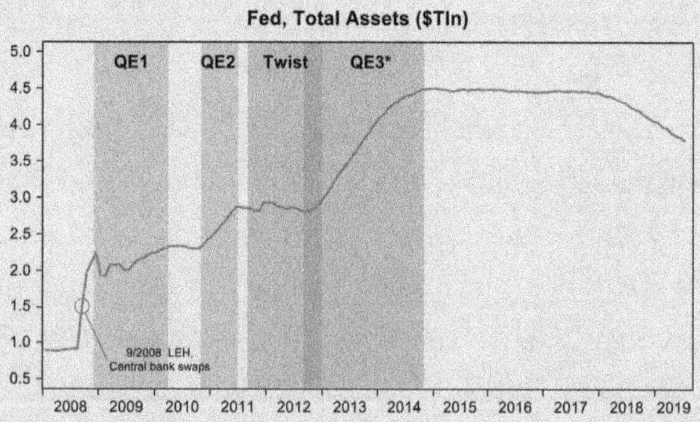

fig 8.2

Source: Macrobond, Mizuho Securities USA, Bloomberg

Federal Reserve Total Assets

An analysis of this country's experience with gold leads us to question the nostalgia that surrounds the gold standard. A detailed look at the historical record highlights that the shift to a fiat currency was not a discussion made by foolhardy politicians. Nor was the United States dogmatically committed to a gold standard since its founding, as some gold advocates would have us believe. Paper money was also in circulation alongside gold coins, even during the periods of a metallic monetary standard in the nineteenth and twentieth centuries. So let's review some significant observations about our historical experience with gold before we discuss the mechanics of a gold standard and the role monetary policy played during the later stage of this period.

IMPORTANT OBSERVATIONS CONCERNING THE GOLD EXPERIENCE

The importance of the below historical observations concerning this country's experience with gold will become increasingly clear as we delve into the mechanics of a gold standard and the role of monetary policy under such a disciplined currency system. The limitations imposed on the flexibility of the money supply will be highlighted when we discuss the financial panics experienced during the classic gold standard period. This discussion will also help explain why it was so difficult to maintain a gold standard, despite the political and general population's interest in adhering to a disciplined approach to managing money supply.

1. Some form of gold standard existed in this country only from 1879 to 1933. Prior to this period, there was technically a bimetallic standard between 1834 and 1862; a fiat standard from 1862 through 1879; and a quasi–gold standard after 1933 until 1971.
2. Even under the gold standard, paper money circulated. Initially, banks issued paper money redeemable in gold. Following the Civil War, paper money was not legal tender, yet it circulated freely. The gold reserves behind the paper money issued were, at the time, never more than a fraction of the paper float.
3. Gold is no guarantee against currency devaluation. The Treasury determines the official value for conversion, but the price of gold in the market could still vary substantially. With free export and import, as well as free coinage, this volatility could and has caused periods of significant devaluation. Domestic inflation could also pressure the conversion rate, as well as gold's "safe-haven" quality.
4. As early as 1853, coins were being minted with less metal than the official conversion rate required, yet they were considered legal tender.
5. The classic gold standard that ended in 1933 was a genuine gold standard, requiring the free export and import of gold along with free coinage and melting back into bullion. Defining the dollar in terms of gold is not a gold standard.

6. The Federal Reserve operated under a gold standard for the first twenty years of its history, as its notes were fully convertible into gold.
7. Policy makers did not orchestrate the move to a fiat currency. Instead, it unfolded by default as macroeconomic conditions made it impossible to maintain the dollar's link to gold. The quasi–gold standard that evolved in 1933 began to break apart in the late 1960s, which culminated with the actions taken by President Nixon in 1971 when he closed the gold window. This decision, by default, shifted the dollar to a free-floating fiat standard.

The Nuts and Bolts of a Gold Standard

Understanding the mechanics of a classical gold standard is critical to appreciating why many still consider this form of monetary regime the ideal standard, and why reinstating it is still discussed in many quarters. The discipline imposed on the origination, distribution, and management of money supply helps ensure increased stability in prices and in exchange rates under a disciplined gold standard. The free flow of gold domestically and internationally provides an automatic mechanism to keep inflation and other imbalances in check. This increases the store-of-value aspect of money as well as the unit of account while facilitating transactions. Additionally, the nuts and bolts of a gold standard are conceptually very easy to understand.

Big negatives are a lack of flexibility in the supply of money and the deflation it often produces to correct imbalances. The quasi–gold standard implemented after 1933 was designed to address these concerns, but at a cost—the tendency for a government to debase its currency in order to boost domestic growth. Academics are quick to point out that a properly managed fiat currency regime can achieve the same price and foreign exchange stability as a classical gold standard, as long as the makers of monetary policy focus on maintaining these long-term goals instead of achieving short-term growth targets.

In a genuine gold standard, the basic monetary unit is specified as a fixed weight and purity of gold. Alexander Hamilton, as the first Secretary of the Treasury, was instrumental in getting the Coinage Act of 1792 through Congress. This legislation defined the dollar as equal to 1.6 grams of gold and set a mint ratio of 15:1 between silver and gold. Because the mint ratio favored silver, the country was initially on a silver standard. By 1834, market conditions led to the first of what would be many devaluations of the dollar. Specifically, the Coinage Act of 1834 cut the gold value of the dollar to 1.5 grams from 1.6 grams and increased the mint ratio to 16:1. This then shifted the country to a de facto gold standard.

A classic gold standard requires the government to offer to freely convert gold bullion into full-bodied gold coins. This policy of unlimited minting is referred to as *free coinage*. As a result, money is created through the public's demand to convert bullion into coins. Another key aspect of a gold standard is that any paper money or token coins that circulate in the economy need to be readily convertible back into gold coin or bullion on demand by either domestic or foreign holders. A common misunderstanding is to assume that under a gold standard, prices are denominated in gold when they are denominated in dollars. Another important misconception is that a gold standard needs to be administered by government. In theory, it may be a market-based system with private mints supplying gold coins, and banks supplying both notes and deposits that are redeemable in gold coins.

In a closed economy, the supply of gold coins is determined by (1) the supply of gold in the economy; and (2) the supply of gold used for nonmonetary purposes (e.g., jewelry, industrial, etc.). The supply of gold in the long run is determined by the opportunity cost of producing gold, or the cost in terms of forgone labor and capital returns in other endeavors. The demand for nonmonetary gold is determined by the purchasing power of gold in relation to other commodities (e.g., silver), while the demand for gold coins is determined by a community's wealth, tastes, and the opportunity cost of holding gold relative to other assets. Competition among gold-producing companies ensures that the purchasing power of gold will equal the opportunity cost of minting the next gold coin.

To understand how this works, let's assume there is a technological advance that raises productivity in nongold sectors of the economy. This results in a rise in economic activity and an increase in the demand for gold coins. The increase in output pushes prices down at the initial level of gold coins in circulation. As prices fall, the output of gold coins will rise as miners increase production and/or consumers monetize non-monetary gold holdings. This results in an increased supply of gold coins, and the initial decline in prices is reversed.

Alternatively, a discovery of new gold reserves, which increases the supply of gold coins, will reduce the purchasing power of money. The resulting shift out of gold coins into non-monetary uses reverses the initial rise in prices that was associated with the initial increase in gold coins in the system. This free flow of gold provides an automatic stabilizer for prices in the economy, and it is this aspect that drives most gold advocates to push for its return.

Extrapolating away from the closed economy model discussed above to a more robust multi-economy system still results in long-term price stability, given that all participants adhere to a classic gold standard. Under such a monetary regime, all countries denominate their currency in terms of specific weight and purity of gold. This fixes the exchange rates between different economies and enables the free flow of gold within an economy and within the system, which assures imbalances are self-corrected. Trade or inflationary imbalances will be corrected (over time) by an automatic balance of payments mechanism described as the *price-specie flow* by David Hume. As in the closed economy model, let's assume there is a technology advance in one country that lowers prices locally.

The fall in domestic prices also lowers the price of exports relative to that of imported goods. This change in the terms of trade will cause foreigners to demand more exported goods and reduce the demand for imported goods. A balance-of-payments surplus will cause gold to flow into the domestic economy, increasing the money supply and reversing the initial drop in prices. This mechanism works in reverse in overseas economies. In the long run, the *price-specie flow* creates price stability globally, as long as all economies in the system employ the gold coin standard or its equivalent.

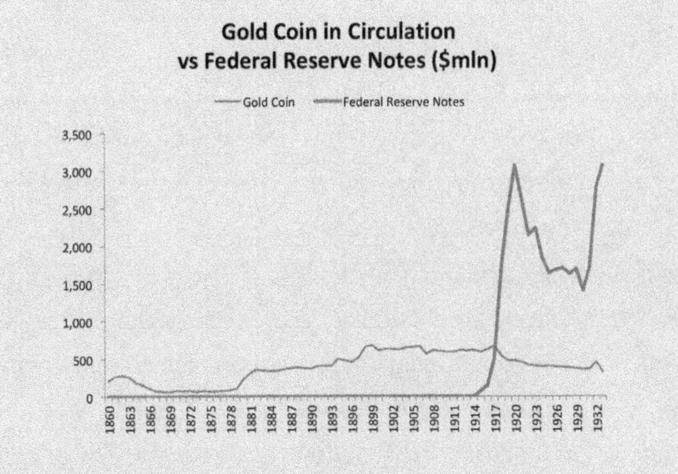

fig 8.3

Gold Coin in Circulation, 1860–1933

The classic gold coin standard discussed above was seldom implemented, and never fully implemented in this country. After Franklin D. Roosevelt signed Executive Order 6102 in 1933, making it illegal for individuals in the United States to own gold, adopting a gold coin standard became impossible. The rigidity imposed on the economy by a classic or true gold coin standard and the deflation caused by the *price-specie flow* also prompted governments to modify the gold standard they adopted in order to economize on the use of physical gold and to shield their economies from external disturbances.

The high resource costs required to maintain a gold coin standard were another reason that substitutes for the classic gold coin standard were developed. These tended to include some form of paper money in lieu of gold coins. Prior to 1933, government-issued paper money, banknotes, and bank deposits were all available in the economy along with gold coins, resulting in a "quasi–gold standard" being in place before World War I. As long as the government maintained a fixed ratio of its notes to gold, and banks were required to keep fixed-ratio gold reserves to their liabilities, the benefits of a gold standard could be maintained. This mixed monetary system meant that a one-dollar equivalent in gold could support multiple paper dollars. A mixed-currency regime among various economies allows for international capital flows to function as an automatic stabilizer to correct imbalances that emerge among members of the system.

Consider the example discussed above in the closed economy model, where the system needs to adjust to an increase in the gold supply. This discovery of a new source of gold leads to a rise in the domestic money supply, which raises domestic prices and lowers money market rates in the short run.

The reduction in domestic interest rates relative to comparable short rates in other economies induces investors to shift funds overseas. The resulting gold flow out of the economy reduces the domestic money supply and, in the process, dampens inflation and pushes domestic short rates back. This stems the outflow of gold and nudges the system back into equilibrium.

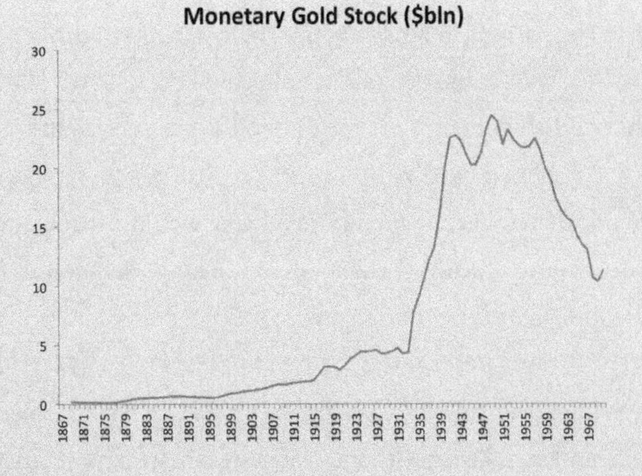

fig 8.4

Monetary Gold Stock

Gold and the Role of Central Banking

Central banks are not necessarily under a classic gold standard. All that is required under the classic gold standard is that a government or private entity maintains the fixed dollar price of gold by buying and selling the commodity in the open market. A central bank's primary mission under a classic gold coin standard was to maintain convertibility of the national currency into gold at the prescribed price. A clear example of a private entity serving as a central bank prior to World War I is the Bank of England, which was established in 1694 as a private institution but served as the government's bank. The United States did not have a central bank prior to World War I, but this situation changed when Congress authorized the creation of the Federal Reserve System in the wake of repeated bank runs. More specifically, a loss in depositor confidence in the viability of a bank would cause depositors to rush to withdraw their funds, causing the bank to fail. We will discuss these bank runs in more detail shortly.

The Federal Reserve was created in December 1913, and its role as the government's bank naturally led the Fed to function as the lender of last resort and the system's primary regulator. Its regional structure enabled it to become the principal clearinghouse for checks and transactions in government debt. The Fed was also authorized by Congress to issue notes backed by the government's debt and was required to redeem these notes for gold on demand. The creation of the Federal Reserve finally led to a unified, national paper currency. Although the Fed did not exist during the US gold standard period, it is still important to understand the role of the central bank under a gold regime by analyzing the experience of other countries.

The principal responsibility of a central bank in an economy functioning under a gold standard is to "play by the rules of the game." Specifically, a central bank is supposed to raise interest rates when gold is leaving the economy and lower rates when gold flows in. Simply doing nothing in the face of substantial gold flows would not be playing by the rules. Studies have found most central banks appear to have taken this aspect of their responsibility seriously prior to 1914. Additionally, central banks during this period would manipulate their gold points, the price they paid relative to what they sold gold for, to hasten necessary adjustments in the market price for the commodity. By raising the price they would pay for gold, the amount of gold flowing into an economy could be increased, and vice versa if they needed to hasten an outflow of gold coins. Banks during this period also held sizable reserves in foreign-denominated financial assets and in foreign exchange. These reserve holdings enabled the central bank to intervene directly in the foreign exchange markets to smooth out excessive or unwanted fluctuations in exchange rates consistent with the bank's gold points.

Central banks used another important tool during this period—the discount policy. Broadly, a discount policy involves any measures employed by the central bank to affect the cost and availability of credit provided to the market. Typically, this tool involved changes in the rates charged on discounts and advances of collateral and/or restricting the access to central bank credit.

Financial Crises under the Rule of Gold

The period between the Civil War and 1913 is known as the Gilded Age. This dynamic period saw rapid economic growth and an expansion of the US financial system. Despite the quasi–gold standard in place, a series of financial accidents marred the economic landscape as speculation went largely unchallenged. Between 1873 and 1913, eight banking panics rumbled through Wall Street and were felt throughout the country. The panics of 1884, 1890, 1899, 1901, and 1908 were principally Wall Street events, while those of 1873, 1893, and 1907 were widespread panics. The 1873 disruption arose from overinvestment in railroads, which squeezed returns relative to robust expectations and led to a boom/bust environment in this key space. A severe financial crisis erupted in 1893 when the gold reserves held by the US Treasury fell below $100 million, down $90 million in just three years. The fear that the government might have to suspend convertibility caused a run on interior banks, as people rushed to withdraw deposits and convert their currency to gold. A recession only added to this panic as loan defaults spiked, especially at smaller regional banks.

The year 1907 saw the first worldwide financial crisis and ultimately led to the creation of the Federal Reserve System in 1913. What made this crisis so important is that it was concentrated in trust companies. These state-chartered intermediaries competed with banks for deposits but were not a big part of the payments system because they tended to have a low volume of checks to clear. As a result, they held a low percentage of cash reserves against deposits (5 percent instead of 25 percent for banks). Their deposits, however, were redeemable for cash, which left the trust companies just as susceptible to a run as a bank. Despite their minor role in the payments system, they were large and important to the financial system. Moreover, trust companies did not require collateral for loans, which had to be repaid at the end of each business day.

Brokers used these loans to purchase securities for themselves and their clients and then used the securities purchased for a call loan, or an overnight loan that facilitated stock purchases. The trust companies filled an important niche in the financial system because banks were prohibited from making uncollateralized loans and from making loans or guaranteeing payment of checks written by brokers on accounts with insufficient funds. These financial institutions provided the liquidity that supported the daily transactions on the New York Stock Exchange (NYSE).

The weaknesses in this structure surfaced on October 16, 1907. Two minor speculators, F. Augustus Heinze and Charles W. Morse, suffered huge losses in a failed attempt to corner the stock of United Copper, a copper mining company. When their bid to manipulate the price of United Copper failed, the banks associated with these speculators (national banks and trust banks) experienced a run on their deposits. The New York Clearing House was successful in stopping the run on Mercantile National Bank (one of its members) but refused to help the trust banks involved, particularly Knickerbocker

Trust. After repeated attempts to rescue Knickerbocker failed, the run on its deposits accelerated, forcing the bank to suspend operations. This intensified the run on trust banks and prompted J. P. Morgan to intercede and stop the run at the Trust Company of America, which was reaching crisis level.

This breakdown in the trust bank system resulted in a spike on the call money rate, or the rate paid on overnight loans using stock collateral offered by the New York Stock Exchange, which rose from 9.5 percent to over 100 percent. Even at this rate, liquidity still dried up and exacerbated the crisis. The meltdown among trust banks ended only after the New York Clearing House committee stepped in and began offering clearinghouse loan certificates to trust banks.

The financial crisis of 1907 also had a severe effect on the real economy, which reverberated overseas. Industrial production is estimated to have tumbled by 17 percent in 1908, while real GDP is estimated to have fallen 12 percent. The loss of economic activity associated with the 1907 crisis would be eclipsed only by the decline caused by the Great Depression. Moreover, the inability of the national banking system to adequately deal with the crisis at nonmember trust banks exposed the need for a national bank regulator and a lender of last resort. This flaw in the banking industry would lead to the creation of the Federal Reserve.

Depression and the End of the Gold Exchange Standard

The evolution of the banking industry, central banking, and the financial system's continued allegiance to gold following World War I reached a critical transition during the Great Depression. The depth of the decline in economic conditions and the view that the gold standard was a critical contributor to the Depression prompted President Roosevelt to end the ability of US citizens to hold monetary gold, and he ordered the exchange of all gold coins, bullion, and gold certificates for Federal Reserve notes. This development technically ended the link between money and gold, even though the government still denominated the value of the dollar in terms of a specific weight and purity of gold. To ease the stress on banks during the Depression, all commercial banks were ordered to exchange their remaining gold reserves for Federal Reserve notes. Banks were also prohibited from exporting gold unless authorized by the Treasury.

These emergency measures, plus a handful of other regulatory changes, amounted to the indefinite suspension of the quasi–gold or gold exchange standard. As such, the exchange value of the dollar floated freely against other major currencies. A new monetary system would not be established until 1936, when the United Kingdom, France, and the United States entered into a Tripartite Monetary Agreement. Under this arrangement, a free flow of gold or foreign exchange was allowed in order to stabilize exchange rates and promote foreign trade without affecting the internal value of the domestic currency.

Once the invasion of Poland pushed Europe into all-out conflict in 1939, the combatants again adopted a fiat currency standard, as they had done during previous conflicts, including World War I. A fiat currency regime allowed these countries to retain control over their gold supplies, which would be needed for security or defense purposes, such as buying military hardware.

After the D-Day invasion turned the tide of the conflict away from the Axis powers, the United States and United Kingdom quickly realized that a postwar financial system would need to be implemented as soon as hostilities ended to avoid financial chaos and help ensure the peace would last this time. As a result, delegates from forty-four allied and associated countries convened in Bretton Woods, New Hampshire, to decide how the world's financial system would look after the war. The Bretton Woods system continued to link the dollar to gold, but in an entirely new manner, and enshrined the US dollar at the center of the new world financial system. This new world order would last only until the 1970s, when it would succumb to a combination of inflationary imbalances and devaluation pressure.

Chapter 9 provides a detailed discussion of the postwar system and why it eventually failed, and it completes our analysis of the role gold played as money in this country.

TIMELINE OF US GOLD STANDARD

Date	*Event*
1834	The United States switched from bimetallic gold and silver to just gold, with the dollar set at $20.67 per ounce of gold. Paper money could still be redeemed for silver.
1900	The Gold Standard Act established gold as the only standard for redeeming paper money.
1913	Congress created the Federal Reserve, and notes issued by the central bank became the national currency with convertibility into gold.
1929	People hoarded gold during the Great Depression. The Fed's attempt to reverse this contraction in money hiked rates, worsening the downturn.
1933	Another run on gold caused President Roosevelt to declare a bank holiday, ending gold convertibility, and he called for all monetary gold to be turned in by citizens, creating the gold reserves at Fort Knox.
1934	The Gold Reserve Act nationalized all gold by ordering the Federal Reserve to turn over its supply of gold to the Treasury in exchange for gold certificates to be used as reserves behind Federal Reserve notes. The dollar was devalued by 40 percent to $35 per ounce of gold.

1936 The United Kingdom, France, and the United States adopted a gold reserve standard to stabilize exchange rates without affecting the internal value of the currency.

1939 The invasion of Poland ignited World War II, and European countries adopted fiat currency regimes.

Chapter 9

The Postwar Monetary System

The seeds of the postwar monetary system were sown even before hostilities ceased. The conference held in Bretton Woods, New Hampshire, from July 1 to 22, 1944, was the culmination of discussions that stretched back to the Atlantic Charter drafted in August 1941 between President Roosevelt and Prime Minister Winston Churchill. This agreement set forth ambitious goals for the postwar world. Specifically, the charter asserted the rights of all nations to equal access to trade and raw materials. Freedom of the seas was also a central pillar of the charter, as was the call for establishing a more permanent system of general security. Building on these principles, with the establishment in 1930 of the Bank for International Settlements (BIS) as a template for multinational organizations, the United Nations Monetary and Financial Conference sought to ensure the mistakes made after World War I were not repeated.

THE OLDEST INTERNATIONAL FINANCIAL INSTITUTION

The BIS was originally intended to help facilitate the settlement of financial obligations that rose out of the Treaty of Versailles that ended World War I. Essentially, the BIS was established as a central banks' bank. The BIS was intended to foster international monetary and financial cooperation and was based in Basel, Switzerland, where it remains today. Although the BIS provided traditional banking services, it only serviced member central banks, which naturally led to today's regulatory aspect of its mission. The BIS also acted as a trustee for the loans made to finance reparations owed after World War I, and was expected to promote central bank cooperation.

The next step in establishing a model for the postwar financial system came in 1936, when the United Kingdom, France, and the United States established a gold reserve standard. A quasi–gold exchange standard had been in place prior to 1933, when Depression-era measures were established—prohibiting US citizens from possessing monetary gold and with the government outlawing the export of gold. By 1936, there was a clear need to stimulate trade in the hope of reviving the global economy, and a new Tripartite Monetary Agreement was implemented among the three reserve currencies of the time. The United Kingdom, France, and the United States agreed to a free flow of gold and foreign exchange to stabilize exchange rates and, as a result, promote increased foreign trade. To facilitate this effort, an Exchange Stabilization Fund was created. This new approach worked well until Germany invaded Poland and the outbreak of World War II prompted the combatants to once again transit to a fiat monetary system. As the war decimated Europe and cemented America's dominance in manufacturing and on the battlefield, the role of the dollar naturally increased at the expense of both the franc and pound. To fund their share of the war effort, France and Britain also transferred the bulk of their monetary gold to the gold bullion depository at Fort Knox, Kentucky.

Realizing a new financial order was needed as soon as hostilities ended prompted serious discussions on both sides of the Atlantic as to what that world should look like. The two key players in driving the process forward were economists John Maynard Keynes of the British Treasury and Harry Dexter White of the US Treasury. Although they had very different visions of the best system for the postwar period, they both agreed on the end goals: stable, liquid financial markets and stable exchange rates in order to promote increased global trade as the means to expand the global economy. Beggar-thy-neighbor policies of the interwar period were regarded as the catalysts for the second conflict.

The philosophical debate between Keynes and White never really took place, despite the merits of Keynes's position. At the end of the day, the practical realities of the US government's dominant position resulted in Harry White's approach being adopted. The dollar took center stage in the new world order, a role it still enjoys today. Unfortunately, the framework advocated by White collapsed in 1971, when the economic reality of inflation in the postwar period rendered the system unworkable.

BANCOR

Keynes proposed an International Clearing Union (ICU) as a measure to regulate the balance of trade. He was concerned that countries with trade deficits would be unable to grow out of their debt servicing costs, and this situation would limit growth in these economies. To avoid this scenario, he envisioned the ICU as a bank with its own currency ("Bancor"), exchangeable into national currencies at a fixed rate. The Bancor would be the unit of account between nations. As such, all trade deficits or surpluses could be measured at a level footing, allowing for easy comparisons across nations.

Each country would also have an overdraft facility in Bancor. If a country exceeded its maximum overdraft, it would be charged interest on the net balance, obliging this country to reduce the value of its currency to prevent capital exports. Moreover, countries with surpluses would also be charged interest at a rate of 10 percent if the surplus was more than half the size of their permitted overdraft. This situation required the surplus country to increase the value of its currency and export capital. If, at year-end, the surplus country's credit exceeded half the allowed overdraft, the surplus would be confiscated. The United States, being the world's largest creditor at the time, was strongly opposed to the Keynes proposal and successfully pushed for a dollar/gold-based system generally referred to as Bretton Woods.

The Gold Parity System of Bretton Woods

The postwar Bretton Woods monetary system not only positioned the US dollar at the center of the world's financial system, it also established a gold parity standard that came into effect with the creation of the International Monetary Fund (IMF) in 1946. Under this standard, every member country defined the value of its currency in terms of gold, and these par values established the exchange rate for foreign transactions. Flexibility was introduced by allowing countries to change their currencies' par value within specified, agreed-upon limits. To ease the cost of correcting imbalances that affect exchange rates, the IMF could provide loans in foreign currencies to members. Gold could also be used to settle international payments, and this aspect of the system would lead to its downfall in 1971.

The new financial model was also supported by the creation of the International Bank for Reconstruction and Development (IBRD), a cooperative owned by its members and intended to help finance the reconstruction of war-torn Europe. The IBRD remains a key function of the World Bank today, but its mission has evolved over the years.

The new gold parity system lasted from 1946 to just 1971, when inflation in the United States and the associated pressure on the dollar led to a run on domestic gold supplies. By 1971, these stresses—the Great Inflation—forced President Nixon to end gold convertibility by foreign governments, shifting the United States to a fiat currency standard.

This chapter builds on the gold standard discussion in Chapter 8 by extending the analysis from 1933 to today. To this end, we will present a detailed discussion of the Bretton Woods system, as well as a review of the economic conditions that led to its eventual failure. We will explain the current fiat money standard, along with the risks imposed by delinking from gold. Our discussion of the risk of debasement helps explain why the allure of gold is still strong today among many participants, and why cryptocurrencies were recently created.

A Lasting Peace Would Need a New Financial System

The attendees at the Bretton Woods conference hoped to establish a global financial system that would avoid a repeat of the mistakes made in the 1920 Treaty of Versailles, which created so much political and economic tension that the world was plunged back into a horrific war just two decades later. In simple terms, the reparations imposed on Germany at the end of World War I were beyond its ability to pay, which meant that many assets on bank balance sheets internationally were unrecoverable. This situation, and an inclination toward isolationism in the United States, sowed the seeds for the Great Depression and the breakdown of the international financial system. The so-called "beggar-thy-neighbor" policies that emerged led to competitive currency devaluations, attempting to increase relative competitiveness. The associated increase in capital flows exacerbated trade and capital account imbalances and increased the risk of renewed hostility.

To ensure this situation would not be repeated, the Allied nations present at Bretton Woods overwhelmingly favored a regulated system of fixed exchange rates, which Harry White believed should be centered on the US dollar being tied to gold. Specifically, a new financial system should rely on a regulated market economy with tight controls on the value of currencies. The aim was to limit speculative international flows in favor of foreign direct investment (FDI). In other words, stimulate the construction of factories overseas rather than manipulate overseas financial markets. The Allied attendees at the 1944 conference believed that to ensure economic stability, governments would need to closely police the production of their currencies and that they would not artificially manipulate their inflation rates.

To this end, Harry White's new system would rest primarily on two new international financial institutions: the International Monetary Fund (IMF) and the International Bank for Reconstruction and Development (IBRD). The new rules of financial engagement sought to encourage an open system of convertible currencies founded on the principles of free trade. What emerged was a "pegged rate" currency model. Members were required to establish a parity of their local currency to the reserve currency, or peg, and to maintain an exchange rate within 1 percent of parity by intervening in the currency market. To bolster confidence in this new system, the US Treasury agreed to link the dollar to gold at a rate of $35 per ounce, establishing the dollar as the peg or reserve currency. Essentially, in the new system, all currencies were linked to the dollar while the dollar was tied to gold. As such, all international transactions would be denominated in dollars. The IMF would be responsible for administering this new system, while the IBRD would finance the reconstruction effort. The five main features of the agreement behind the IMF were the following:

1. An adjustable, pegged foreign exchange system where exchange rates were pegged indirectly through the US dollar

to gold. Governments were to alter their exchange rates only to correct fundamental imbalances.

2. Member countries pledged to make their currencies convertible for trade and related current account transactions.
3. Governments could address sustained trade-related imbalances by adjusting their currency peg by up to 10 percent of its initial level without objection from the IMF. Beyond that, approvals would be required. The IMF could not force a country to undo a change made to their relative value of its currency but could deny access to IMF resources.
4. All member countries were required to subscribe to the IMF's capital. Membership in the IBRD was conditional on being a member of the IMF.
5. Voting rights in both the IMF and the IBRD were (and still are) proportional to a country's capital contribution. These contributions were set as 25 percent in gold and 75 percent in their own currency.

In practice, IMF members experiencing a current account deficit with insufficient reserves could borrow foreign currency in accordance with its quota. Each member could withdraw up to 25 percent of its quota immediately in the case of payment problems. After this initial withdrawal, each member country could request a loan of foreign currency. Fund members were required to repay loans within eighteen months to five years. To avoid countries going too deeply into debt, the IMF could exercise surveillance on members and make recommendations to correct imbalances.

The flexibility built into the IMF system through the allowable adjustments in the peg and the availability of IMF loans was designed to avoid the forced deflation and increased unemployment imposed by a gold standard on a country with a chronic, trade-related imbalance. The IMF was capitalized with $10 billion and was expected to make loans and underwrite private loans to speed the postwar recovery. To this end, the IBRD could also issue securities to raise additional funds to increase its ability to make loans to members. The interest spread earned and the return on its capital would fund operations and increase capital over time.

Besides the IMF and the IBRD, the Allies at Bretton Woods sought to end economic nationalism by lowering or eliminating barriers to trade and capital flows. These initiatives were embodied in the proposed International Trade Organization (ITO) agreed to at the UN Conference on Trade and Employment held in Havana, Cuba, in March 1948. Political considerations killed the ITO in the US Senate and a less ambitious General Agreement on Tariffs and Trade (GATT) was passed. In 1995, it morphed into the World Trade Organization (WTO), which is still charged with administering the principles of GATT and extending them where possible.

Achilles' Heel

The IMF became operative in 1946 and President Truman appointed Harry White as its first executive director. Almost immediately, the unforeseen developments of the postwar period began to stress the system White put in place at Bretton Woods. Postwar capitalism suffered from a huge dollar shortage. After the war, the United States was running a huge balance of trade surplus and the country's reserves reflected this imbalance. Even though all nations wanted to buy US exports, dollars had to be recycled overseas. Essentially, the United States would need to run a financial account deficit in order to offset the trade surplus. To this end, the United States could either build plants overseas or donate money to foreign nations. Because US technology was innovative, increasing imports was not a viable option. Therefore, foreign direct investment (FDI) had to expand, as did foreign aid programs, as it quickly became clear that the modest credit facilities of the IMF and the IBRD were insufficient to deal with the scope of the dollar shortage. This initiative was formalized in the European Recovery Program, aka the Marshall Plan. This Truman-era program provided large-scale financial and economic aid for rebuilding through grants rather than loans. As a result, the United States deliberately encouraged a large capital outflow of dollars from 1947 until 1958, while also running a balance of payments deficit from 1950 onward with the intent of providing liquidity for the international economy. Aid to Europe and Japan was designed to rebuild productivity and export capacity. The idea was that this aid would, in the long run, increase markets for US exports.

The dollar shortage would be just the first of a string of problems that would stress the postwar financial model designed at Bretton Woods. The Cold War period and the stresses imposed in the wake of excess demand would eventually lead to failure of the gold parity or dollar peg systems.

Although the US Treasury held sufficient gold reserves at the outset of the Bretton Woods system, the expanding global economy of the 1950s and 1960s required more liquidity than the expansion in gold stock afforded. At the end of the war, the United States held an estimated $26 billion in gold, or 65 percent of the world's supply. With the postwar Stalin regime opting not to participate in the Bretton Woods financial system, the largest source of new gold was locked behind the Iron Curtain. This weakness in the system was obvious in the latter half of the 1950s as the US balance of payments swung into negative territory. To address this shift in fortunes, the Eisenhower administration began to fall back on protectionist measures, including import quotas on oil and other restrictions of trade flows. However, the 1958 recession stopped additional anticompetitive measures from being advanced.

The next developments to undermine the fundamentals of the Bretton Woods system were the escalation of the Vietnam War and the Johnson "Great Society" experiment. This combination of government policies deteriorated the country's fiscal position and put a significant strain on the economy precisely when the baby boom generation was entering the labor force. The result was a sharp decline in productivity and a spike in unit labor costs. Rising wage demands and union power resulted in cost of living adjustments (COLA) being built into contracts, and a wage-price spiral took hold of the economy. The emergence of the Organization of Petroleum Exporting Countries

(OPEC) and escalating oil prices complicated the economic landscape and resulted in a period of rising unemployment and rising inflation. This period of "stagflation" would stress the fundamental underpinnings of the Bretton Woods system.

The inflation that emerged put extreme pressure on the dollar and pushed gold prices in the open market above the $35-per-ounce conversion price dictated by the dollar peg. The greater the gap between gold in the open market and the convertibility price, the more incentive there was for countries to exchange their accrued trade-related dollar reserve holdings for gold. A continuous balance of payments deficit was necessary to keep the financial system flush with US dollars, which ensured sustained growth, but over time, these same deficits would undermine confidence in the dollar and erode its status as the reserve currency.

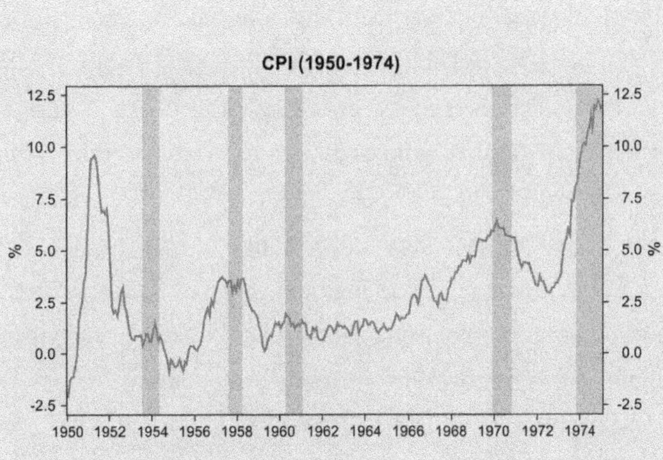

***fig* 9.1**

Source: Macrobond, Mizuho Securities USA, BLS

CPI Year-Over-Year: 1950–1974

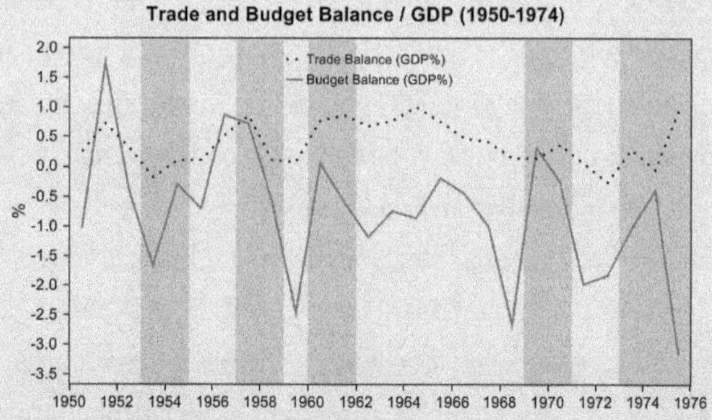

fig **9.2**

Source: Macrobond. Mizuho Securities USA, US Department of Treasury

Trade and Budget Balance as a Percent of GDP: 1950–1974

To counter the drain on US gold reserves caused by domestic inflation and growing trade imbalances, eight IMF members established the London Gold Pool in November 1961, attempting to defend the Bretton Woods gold conversion price of $35 per ounce. The theory behind the gold pool was relatively simple: Spikes in the price of gold would be controlled by having a pool of gold to sell in the open market; when prices dipped below $35 per ounce, the pool would purchase gold in the market to support the conversion price.

Although the gold pool temporarily eased pressures on the price of gold, the domestic supply of gold had been squeezed significantly and, by 1967, a run on the dollar further exacerbated conditions. Trade deficits and inflation problems proved to be more stubborn than economists had expected. In a failed attempt to correct this situation, the Johnson administration undertook a series of measures designed to stem the outflow of gold and boost US exports in January 1968. By March 1968, a run on gold caused the gold pool to collapse, as members refused to keep defending the official price of $35 per ounce.

Special Drawing Right, a new reserve asset. The downward pressure on the dollar relative to gold proved to be a key global policy issue. In the late 1960s, the Fed began to follow a very conservative policy of restricting the flow of dollars in the financial markets, prompting the long December 1969 to November 1970 recession. This restrictive Fed policy and the Cold War's adverse effect on the availability of gold in the West created a concern among IMF members that a shortage of available reserves was likely to emerge. This situation is generally referred to as the Triffin dilemma, or a condition where the domestic and international pressures on the reserve currency require contradictory policy responses by the reserve currency's central bank.

To ease this supply concern, the IMF developed a new reserve asset called a Special Drawing Right (SDR). The SDR is not a currency, but a claim on currency held by the IMF, and was allotted to members based on their contribution to the fund. Initially, one SDR was valued at $1 or 0.888671 gram of gold. Shortly after the IMF's first allocation of $9.3 billion in

SDRs, the Fed shifted course to revive the economy. Escalation of the Vietnam War added to political pressure on domestic policy makers to support the recovery. This increased the supply of US dollars in global markets, and the immediate need for SDRs faded.

Over time, events such as the Latin American debt crisis and the 2007 financial crisis would revive interest in SDRs, leading to additional allocations totaling $215.5 billion to date. Following the breakdown of Bretton Woods, the SDR was redefined as a basket of sixteen currencies. Between July 1974 and December 1980, the basket comprised just five key currencies: the US dollar (USD), the Deutsche mark (DM), the French franc (FRF), the British pound (GBP), and the Japanese yen (JPY). Following the introduction of the euro in January 1999, the SDR was again redefined as a basket of just four currencies: the US dollar, the euro, the British pound, and the Japanese yen. The current composition of the SDR includes the Chinese yuan (CNY) as of October 2016.

By 1970, the United States had seen its gold coverage deteriorate from 55 percent to 22 percent of the paper currency outstanding. This forced the US Congress to repeal the 25 percent requirement of gold backing the dollar, technically ending the Bretton Woods era. However, it was not until August 1971, when President Nixon closed the gold window, that there was one final attempt to reform the international monetary system.

The Smithsonian Agreement of August 1971 was an agreement between the G10 countries designed to rebalance the Bretton Woods system. The United States pledged to peg the dollar at $38 an ounce with a 2.25 percent trading band, while the other parties to the agreement promised to appreciate their currencies against the dollar to ease the stress on the US gold reserves. Additionally, the IMF's SDRs would be used to balance the international payments system instead of gold. This last-ditch attempt failed largely because the Federal Reserve and the US government were more concerned about rising domestic unemployment than the depreciating dollar. As a result, low domestic interest rates caused a continued outflow of dollars from the United States, and the open market price of gold continued to rise. By 1973, the stresses were too great, and several G10 countries opted to let their currency float relative to the dollar. In 1976, the Bretton Woods system officially ended with the formal ratification of the Jamaica Accords. This agreement, ratified by a committee made up of IMF board members, allowed the price of gold to float with respect to the dollar and other currencies. Technically, this had been the case since the Nixon shock of 1971, but it was not official until the 1976 Accords.

Fear of the Unknown

The end of the Bretton Woods system ushered in a new chapter in global monetary history. Many economists and politicians were opposed to the new fiat structure. Their concern centered on the ability of governments to debase the value of new paper money, and history is rife with examples of such behavior.

The current debate among the more left-leaning Democratic candidates over Modern Monetary Theory (MMT) is an example of why the so-called "gold bugs" still long for a return to some form of gold standard. They fear that politicians will debase the currency in order to redistribute wealth from creditors to debtors by means of accelerating inflation. The recent political and academic discussions surrounding MMT can be viewed as evidence that this concern is well placed. MMT asserts that a country that funds in its own currency should not worry about deficit spending, since it technically can't default on its debt. Although the central bank can always print money backed by debt, allowing the government to meet its existing financial obligations, this could still be highly inflationary. (This issue will come up again in a later section.)

There are two obvious examples of government policy designed to deliberately debase the currency. The first was the Weimar Republic in Germany, which lasted fifteen years, from 1918 to 1933. In the aftermath of World War I, Germany lost its richest farmland, and its industrial base was limited by the peace accords. The reparations demanded by the Allies were unreasonable and, as a result, the government turned on the printing presses and tried to hyperinflate out of its problems.

In the end, this tactic failed, and the National Socialist German Workers' Party, or Nazi Party, came to power.

More recently, hyperinflation in Zimbabwe is another clear example of a government exploiting its ability to print money under a fiat model. Redistribution efforts by the government began shortly after the country's involvement in the Second Congo War and included excessive money growth and land confiscation. Inflation began to accelerate and, at its peak, is estimated to have hit an unbelievable rate of 79.6 billion percent a month before the printing stopped in 2009.

In the next chapter we will discuss how a fiat monetary system works and review its history dating back to 1000 CE in China. This will afford us the opportunity to better understand why it is so important that the control of monetary policy be in the hands of an independent central bank rather than being controlled by elected officials. Essentially, history shows that the promise of short-term economic benefits tends to overwhelm the benefits to the economy in the long run, as politicians are naturally worried about being reelected.

Chapter 10

Full Faith and Credit

The common theme that keeps showing up throughout our analysis of money is that no established monetary standard has survived the test of time, but the discipline imposed by gold has been desired throughout time. However, the automatic stabilizer built into this monetary regime, which helps explains its longevity, also tends to produce socially unacceptable consequences. The deflationary contractions imposed on an economy that runs either with persistent trade or inflationary imbalances are the very aspects that gold standard policy makers wish to avoid when implementing alternative currency regimes. As such, gold coins were often augmented with silver coins and/or paper money backed by gold, which gave an economy increased flexibility to grow and avoid painful economic adjustments such as rising interest rates and joblessness. This increased flexibility, however, comes with potentially a very high price: the risk of currency debasement and inflation. History has many examples of currency debasement going back as far as 60 CE, when Emperor Nero reduced the precious metal content of the denarius by 10 percent to increase the supply of money. Money-induced inflation is often cited as one of the reasons behind the fall of the Roman Empire.

The search for a truly flexible, but disciplined, monetary system has led us to today's fiat monetary regime. The explosive growth in the global economy following World War II, the social pressures this growth unleashed, and the limited supply of gold in the Western Hemisphere combined to sink the Bretton Woods dollar-pegged reserve currency system. Remember, this system lasted just a quarter-century, until President Nixon closed the gold window on August 15, 1971. This politically expedient decision technically ended the Bretton Woods system and moved the dollar to a fiat standard, where it remains today.

To better understand how a fiat monetary system functions, it is useful to view money as a financial asset for the holder and a liability of society. Since paper money has no intrinsic value of its own, the liability of society can be used to explain why people have a demand for money under a fiat standard. In this chapter, we will discuss how its value is determined, in contrast to other asset classes, and we will look at the biggest risk associated with fiat money, its debasement, and how this process leads to inflation.

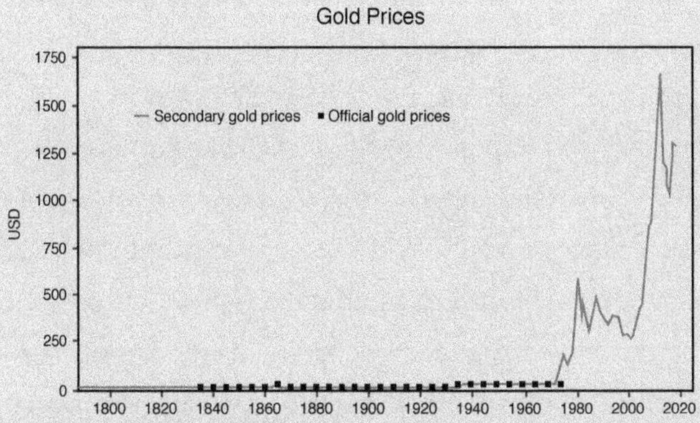

fig 10.1

Source: Macrobond, Mizuho Securities USA

Gold Prices (Official US Gold Price vs. Secondary Market Price)

All Paper Money Is Not Fiat Money

In the past several chapters we have looked at the various forms of commodity-based money and discussed the mechanics behind each, particularly as they relate to US economic history. We discussed the period when the United States was functioning under a hard currency standard, or a gold/silver coin standard. The limitations imposed by the supply of precious metals in the economy and the shifting relative value between these base metals were also discussed, along with how this further complicated the mechanics of a precious metals standard. The forced economic adjustment of the *price-specie flow* was another reason paper money was eventually added to the mix and a gold exchange model was implemented. The addition of paper money increased the flexibility of the monetary system but still imposed significant adjustment costs on the economy when imbalances arose. To avoid excessive printing of paper money under a gold exchange standard, the Federal Reserve was established to regulate the supply of paper money in the economy. Because US domestic manufacturing was left untouched by World War II while Europe and Asia required massive reconstruction, the dollar became the world's reserve currency under the Bretton Woods dollar/gold peg shortly after the Allied victory.

Under Bretton Woods, the value of the dollar was pegged to gold, and all other IMF member countries tied their currencies to gold and the dollar. Physical gold would still be used to settle official international accounts, but with most of the world's supply of gold held in US vaults, the dollar became the reserve currency. Lingering rigidities inherent in this system and the conflicts of interest confronting the Fed under this new monetary regime quickly (in less than 30 years) led to its demise. Specifically, the dollar's role as the reserve currency put the Fed into the difficult (and, at times, impossible) position of having to set monetary policy in the face of conflicting domestic and international needs. Politically, it was clear that domestic considerations tended to win out over international needs, and the result was a rapid acceleration in inflation and a devaluation of the dollar. The stress exerted on the currency came to a head in the early 1970s, resulting in the Nixon shock, or the closing of the gold window. The shift to a fiat monetary system was officially complete by 1978.

While the origins of paper money can be traced back to the Tang Dynasty in China, to around 618 to 907 CE, fiat money was first introduced in this country during the Civil War when the North issued paper script, called greenbacks, in order to save its precious metal reserves for overseas trade, which funded its war effort. The government in the South did the same, but after the war this paper currency was worthless. Later on, we will discuss how the excessive issuance of greenbacks represents the first politically motivated currency debasement and how it soured the desire of many in government to allow a national banking system to develop. It was not until 1913, when the Federal Reserve was established, that a US central bank became a preeminent component of our financial system, even though Alexander Hamilton, the first Treasury secretary, saw the need for a government-sponsored bank as early as the late 1700s.

Asset vs. Liability Approach

Fiat currency models were introduced in Europe during World War I and again during World War II. Even though we have been functioning under such a model since 1971, there are still those who long to return to the rule of gold. Under a fiat monetary standard, money is a financial asset that is not unlike a share of stock. Money represents a proportional claim on the future output of society, that is, a debt instrument. The holders of money, on the other hand, view the value of this asset as they would a corporate equity. A share of common stock is a claim on a company's expected future stream of earnings. Assets derive their value either from their physical properties or from their contractual properties.

Fiat money, the bills and notes we carry in our pockets, is a legal liability of the government and is a contingent claim, or another form of government debt. Essentially, money is a liability of society/government that represents the people in a society. It is also like an equity asset, in that it is a proportional claim on the future output of society, much like equity is a claim on a company's future earnings. By focusing on the liability side of money, it becomes easier to understand why it has value even if it has no intrinsic value of its own.

Where economists traditionally view money as an asset that provides value to the holder, that value is as a medium of exchange, a unit of measurement, and/or a store of value. By looking at money as a liability of society, it is easy to see why it has value and what factors affect its value.

Specifically, the liability approach has several advantages relative to the asset approach adopted by most economists. Defining money as a proportional claim on society's future output suggests it derives its value from the implied contract it represents. This definition also allows us to attach a value to bank deposits, since deposits represent a claim to money. As a claim on society's future output, the value of fiat money depends on an economy's long-term economic expectations.

Moreover, this definition provides a framework for how to value one country's currency relative to that of another.

Essentially, the value of money should be positively correlated with expected long-term, real growth and negatively correlated with inflation (or, in other words, in the wake of an increase in the supply of money printed by the Fed). Rising long-term real growth expectations imply that any given dollar's proportional share of future output should be higher, raising its value, with all other things being equal. Rising inflation expectations mean the real value of a dollar will be worth less in the future, leading to a lower current value. Viewing money as a financial liability of society and an asset to the holder brings the expected real return of other financial assets into the valuation calculation. Rising real interest rates suggest the future benefit from money will rise and so will its value to the holder. Alternatively, the relative value of different currencies will depend on relative growth, inflation, and asset return differentials.

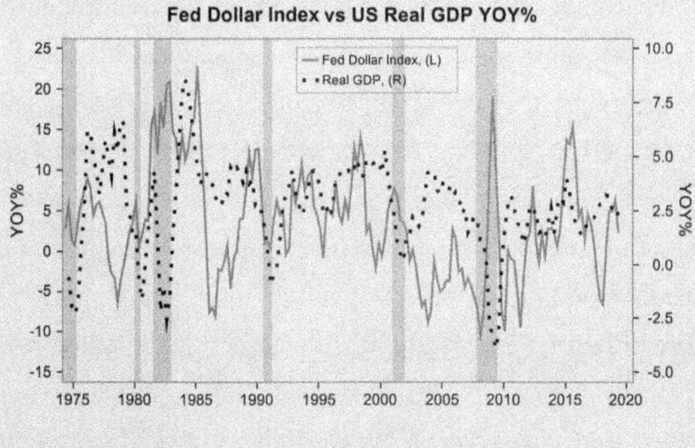

fig 10.2

Source: Macrobond, Mizuho Securities USA, Bloomberg, US Federal Reserve System, BEA

Federal Dollar Index vs. Real GDP (Year-Over-Year)

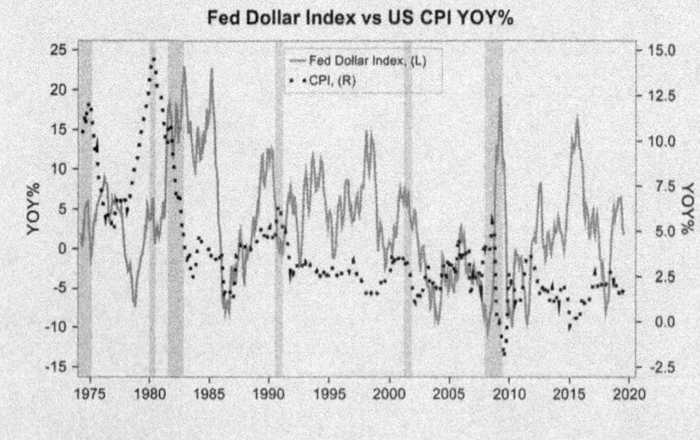

fig 10.3

Source: Macrobond, Mizuho Securities USA, Bloomberg, US Federal Reserve System, BLS

Federal Dollar Index vs. US CPI

The value of the US dollar relative to other currencies depends on the relative difference in expectations on the future value of societies' output. Specifically, the dollar will rise in value relative to other currencies if the outlook for real GDP in the United States exceeds that of other countries. Inflation differentials also determine the relative value of the dollar. The country with the highest rate of inflation will have the weakest currency valuation. Relative real financial market returns will also affect the value of the dollar relative to other currencies. The relative value of money also depends on the differentials in perceived risk between currencies, the perceived stability of the government, and the strength of the rule of law in the country.

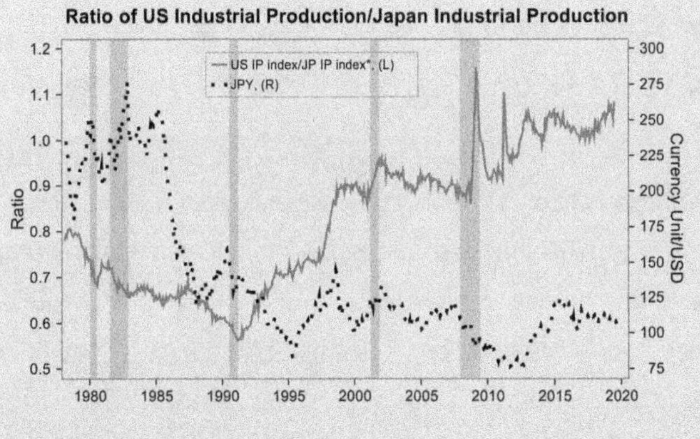

fig 10.4

Source: Macrobond, Mizuho Securities USA, Japan MITI, FRB

Ratio of US Industrial Production/Japan Industrial Production vs. Yen/$

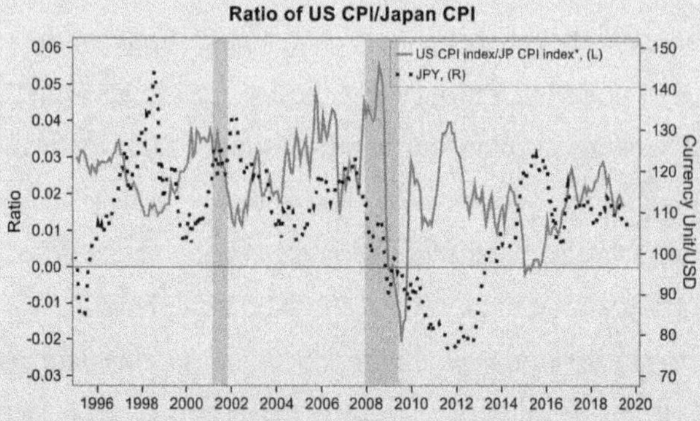

fig 10.5

Source: Macrobond, Mizuho Securities USA, Japan Statistics Bureau, BLS

Ratio US CPI/Japan CPI vs. Yen/Dollar

Measuring Money Is No Easy Task

Our discussion of money so far has generally assumed a very limited set of assets. Under a precious metal standard, the coins minted of gold and/or silver were initially all that needed to be considered. As things shifted to a gold exchange standard, alternative forms of money were added. Token coins that had a limited content of the precious metals were created, as was paper money, all of which were convertible into gold (and, at times, silver) on demand. The growing banking industry added additional forms of money (bank deposits) to the mix. As discussed earlier in this chapter, viewing money as a claim on society's future output allows us to attach a value to bank deposits because they are a claim on money, which explains why people hold bank deposits (a liability of the bank) as assets. This broadening list of assets held as money, or more precisely near money, has led to alternative measures of money.

The aggregating approach to measuring money was motivated by a desire to calculate a measure of money that correlates best with money's role in macroeconomic theory and with theories concerning the demand for money. The earliest of these aggregates were referred to as M0 (M zero) and the monetary base. M0 was defined as the sum of paper money outstanding, Federal Reserve notes, and the coins in circulation. This aggregate essentially measures money that can be immediately used for transactions. Monetary base, on the other hand, consists of currency in circulation (M0), as well as currency stored in bank vaults plus commercial bank reserves on deposit with the Federal Reserve. In our fractional reserve banking system, the monetary base is called "high-powered" money, or the base from which banks can expand their asset and liability base. When money is deposited in a commercial bank, the bank is required to hold a percentage of the deposit as a reserve against potential withdrawals, and the rest can be used to make loans that expand the money supply. The inclusion of vault cash and reserve balances held at the Fed are the two additional assets included in the monetary base that are not included in M0.

The next, more inclusive aggregate that economists at the

Fed compiled was M1. This aggregate builds on M0, not the monetary base, as do all broader aggregates. M1 consists of currency, paper and coins, printed by the Federal Reserve and/or minted by the Treasury, plus demand deposits and other checkable deposits held by banks. The other checkable deposit category includes assets such as Negotiable Orders of Withdrawal accounts (NOW accounts are checking accounts that pay interest) plus travelers' checks. M1, at one point, was broken into two components: M1A and M1B. M1A was essentially M0 excluding demand deposits held by foreign banks and foreign official institutions. M1B was M1A plus NOW accounts and automatic transfer service (ATS) accounts, which were demand deposits that were swept into overnight savings accounts at the end of each business day so the balance could earn interest income. M1B also included ATS at thrifts, credit union share drafts, and deposits at mutual savings banks.

The addition of more near-money assets in M1B results in a series of broader aggregate measures being compiled. The only one of these broader aggregates ever seriously considered by the Federal Reserve as a signal of future inflation pressures was M2. This broader aggregate includes overnight repurchase agreements issued by commercial banks, overnight euro dollar deposits held by nonbank US residents, money market mutual fund shares, and savings and small-time deposits at all depository institutions. Additional measures such as M3, M4, and M5 have also been compiled in the past, in addition to a very broad measure of liquidity in the economy called L. None of these were ever found to be useful in forecasting real growth or inflation, as they tended to be heavily influenced by portfolio decisions made by households and corporations rather than for transition needs.

Monetary aggregates took center stage in monetary policy decisions beginning in 1979, when Fed Chairman Paul Volcker rejected Keynesian macro policy for the monetary approach championed by Milton Friedman. This theory, as discussed earlier, suggests that an expansive monetary policy will have only a limited long-term effect on real GDP, but will result in higher inflation over time. The rapid acceleration in inflation experienced during the 1970s in the wake of rapidly rising crude oil prices and sharply declining labor productivity led the Fed to begin targeting money as a means of regaining control over inflation and hopefully ending stagflation. This dramatic shift in policy began in October 1979 and led to the Fed establishing annual target cones for M1. As this aggregate moved within its target, the Fed either tightened or eased monetary policy, attempting to bring down excessive money growth or bolster growth to achieve its long-term inflation target.

Target Growth Cones for the Monetary and Credit Aggregates (Monetary Aggregate Target Cone, 1980–1993)

			Target and Monitoring Ranges	
Date Established	Base Period	Span	M1	M2
Feb. 80	79Q4	79Q4 – 80Q4	4.0 – 6.5 (M1B)	6.0 – 9.0
Feb. 81	80Q4	80Q4 – 81Q4	3.5 – 6.0 (M1B)	6.0 – 9.0
Feb. 82	81Q4	81Q4 – 82Q4	2.5 – 5.5	6.0 – 9.0
Feb. 83	83 Feb/Mar	83 Feb/Mar – 83Q4	–	7.0 – 10.0
Feb. 83	82Q4	82Q4 – 83Q4	4.0 – 8.0	–
Jul. 83	83Q2	83Q2 – 83Q4	5.0 – 9.0	NC
Jan. 84	83Q4	83Q4 – 84Q4	4.0 – 8.0	6.0 – 9.0
Feb. 85	84Q4	84Q4 – 85Q4	4.0 – 7.0	6.0 – 9.0
Jul. 85	85Q2	85Q2 – 85Q4	3.0 – 8.0	NC
Feb. 86	85Q4	85Q4 – 86Q4	3.0 – 8.0	6.0 – 9.0
Feb. 87	86Q4	86Q4 – 87Q4	NS	5.5 – 8.5
Feb. 88	87Q4	87Q4 – 88Q4	NS	4.0 – 8.0
Feb. 89	88Q4	88Q4 – 89Q4	NS	3.0 – 7.0
Feb. 90	89Q4	89Q4 – 90Q4	NS	3.0 – 7.0
Jul. 90	89Q4	89Q4 – 90Q4	NS	NC
Feb. 91	90Q4	90Q4 – 91Q4	NS	2.5 – 6.5
Feb. 92	91Q4	91Q4 – 92Q4	NS	2.5 – 6.5
Feb. 93	92Q4	92Q4 – 93Q4	NS	2.0 – 6.0
Jul. 93	92Q4	92Q4 – 93Q4	NS	1.0 – 5.0

NC: Not Changed
NS: None Specified

fig 10.6

Source: Richard G. Anderson and Kenneth A. Kavajecz, March/April 1994, A Historical Perspective on the Federal Reserve's Monetary Aggregates: Definition, Construction, and Targeting

Unfortunately, the decision to target money had important and unforeseen consequences that eventually led to the need to abandon this approach to monetary policy. Specifically, the increased volatility in short-term interest rates accelerated the pace of financial engineering, which increasingly blurred the lines between transactions and savings balances, rendering the aggregates ineffective in determining the key macro variables of growth and inflation. As a result, the Fed abandoned its money supply experiment just fifteen years after having implemented it, due to the breakdown in a key assumption—that the velocity of money tended to be relatively stable. The new approach adopted by the Fed would return to the Keynesian model of targeting short-term rates, but this time with a mandate to achieve inflation stability. The risks imposed by this shift in the approach to policy will become evident in the next section, where we discuss currency debasement.

What Has Gone Wrong, and What Could Go Wrong, with a Fiat Monetary Regime?

The shift from a US dollar tied to gold, to a claim on the future output of the economy, occurred under extreme duress. As discussed earlier, the Bretton Woods gold-peg standard collapsed after just a few decades because global excessive macroeconomic demand for goods and services, combined with an expanded social contract under Johnson's Great Society experiment, the Vietnam War, and back-to-back spikes in energy prices, resulted in a rapid acceleration in inflation that eventually transformed into a previously unknown development called stagflation. This combination of accelerating inflation and rising joblessness had huge domestic and international ramifications.

Domestically, stagflation became political quicksand, which pulled the Carter administration down and saw a sweep by Ronald Reagan and the Republicans in the 1980 election. Internationally, this situation caused a high degree of stress within the Bretton Woods system as the dollar pushed lower and gold prices pushed well above the official transaction prices. As demand for the government's gold stock increased, the very fabric of the Bretton Woods system became increasingly stressed until it broke in August 1971. In the wake of these events, President Nixon ended gold convertibility, effectively breaking the link between gold and the dollar. The economic pain that had to be inflicted before this decision could be reached reflected a deep-seated fear among policy makers that allowing the currency to float would lead to a financial disaster. Fear of a loss in confidence in the currency kept policy makers from moving to a fiat model until there was no alternative. Fear that a fiat system would lead to a rapid debasement of the currency played a key role in the long-delayed decision.

Debasement can be defined as the practice of lowering the absolute and/or relative value of a currency. In a commodity currency, reducing the precious metal content of the coins in circulation can do this. There are several historical examples of governments that deliberately debased their currency to generate inflation and reduce the cost of servicing debt. Debt tends to be denominated in nominal terms, creating an incentive for governments to incite inflation by debasing their currency, and in the process, lowering the real cost of servicing the debt. History is rife with this type of behavior. A fiat monetary regime is much easier to implement than a commodity-based currency.

Under a hard currency standard, debasement typically

takes the form of clipping precious metal from existing coins, reducing their gold or silver content. Alternatively, older coins are recalled and replaced with coins containing less of the precious metals. An example of this goes back to ancient times and can be found in Europe and Asia, suggesting it is hard to avoid the temptation. In fact, economists refer to the adulteration of England's currency under Henry VIII and Edward VI as the Great Debasement, principally because this was such an important event in the country's long financial history. To pay for Henry's lavish lifestyle and to fund wars with France and Scotland, the gold purity in English coins was reduced from 23 to 20 karats, and the silver content was cut from 92.5 percent to just 25 percent.

More modern examples include the hyperinflation orchestrated by the Weimar Republic in the wake of Germany's difficulty in dealing with World War I reparations imposed by the Treaty of Versailles. To pay the large costs imposed by the victors and to pay back the money borrowed to fund the war effort, the government turned on the printing presses and the German mark collapsed—with the exchange rate value falling from 7.9 to 48 marks by late 1919. This currency devaluation resulted in hyperinflation and helped bring the Nazi Party to power from its very humble beginnings in 1920. More recently, hyperinflation in Zimbabwe in the late 1990s is another example of a fiat money being debased to deal with adverse conditions created by the government—in this case, its involvement in the Second Congo War.

Domestic Examples of Debasing the Currency

Debasement of the currency has been experienced in this country more than once during and after important historical developments. To fund the Revolutionary War, the Continental Congress began issuing paper money in 1775, known as the continental, in denominations from one-sixth of a dollar to 80-dollar notes. It is estimated that upwards of $241 million was eventually issued, resulting in a significant reduction in their value. By 1778, a continental retained anywhere from one-fifth to one-seventh of its face value. The currency continued to devalue through 1780, when continentals were worth just one-fortieth of their face value. By the early 1790s, after the ratification of the Constitution, holders of continentals could exchange them for Treasury bonds at 1 percent of their face value. This devaluation was effectively a tax on citizens to pay for the war.

Less than a hundred years later, the experience with the continental was ready to be repeated, this time during the Civil War. President Lincoln understood the importance of money during a war, and he appointed Salmon Chase as Secretary of the Treasury. Chase was authorized to act on all matters pertaining to the country's finances. Unfortunately, both the president and Chase underestimated the length of the war and its cost. The extent of this miscalculation became clear very early on, and the government's limited income from tariffs and excise taxes soon needed to be subsidized with bank-related borrowing. The interest expense demanded by New York banks spiraled upward toward 36 percent, forcing a change in the means of financing the war effort. To address this situation, in 1861 Congress authorized the printing of $50 million worth of demand notes that would be called greenbacks, due to the bright green ink used on the back of the notes. These demand notes were initially discounted to gold, but because they were fully redeemable, they were soon being exchanged at par.

Although greenbacks were not legal tender initially, they could be used to pay customs duties. These notes became legal tender in 1862. Because the notes used to pay customs duties were taken out of circulation, by 1863 there was insufficient liquidity to meet the government's mounting obligations. A more dramatic approach by the government was required. The result was issuance of a nonconvertible paper currency that would be considered legal tender and could be used to pay soldiers and buy materials for the war effort. On February 25, 1862, Congress passed the first Legal Tender Act, which provided for the issuance of $150 million of these new US notes. As the war progressed and the supply of greenbacks expanded, their value relative to gold plunged to a low of 258 greenbacks to $100 of gold coins. This decline was associated with the Union Army's struggle to take the Confederate stronghold of Richmond, Virginia. When the war ended and Congress limited the supply of greenbacks to just $50 billion, the currency recovered to 150 greenbacks to $100 in gold. By 1878, greenbacks returned to par with gold as Congress passed legislation making them fully convertible.

These examples of how the US government debased the currency, when conditions called for a fiat monetary regime, lingered in the memory of economists and policy makers following World War II, which explained why Harry White pushed so hard for a dollar/gold-peg system at the Bretton Woods conference. Without an anchor, there was concern that either the financial system would simply collapse or inflation would spiral out of control.

Worst Fears Realized

It was generally understood that a strict gold coin or bullion standard limited the economy's ability to grow faster than the supply of the precious metal. Moreover, the built-in adjustment process designed to correct any imbalances in the economy could also lead to undesirable deflationary pressures and rising unemployment. A fiat monetary regime, on the other hand, ran the risk of deliberate manipulation by the government to debase the value of the currency through inflation. Inflation is a nonlegislated transfer of wealth from creditors to borrowers through devaluation of savings balances. Moreover, a stable currency is seen as vital for the growth of trade as a means of improving the living standard of those who participated. By placing the dollar at the center of the new financial system, and pegging the dollar to gold, Bretton Woods was supposed to create the right mix of discipline and flexibility that was needed to allow the global economy to grow enough to speed reconstruction, but also to keep excesses from accumulating.

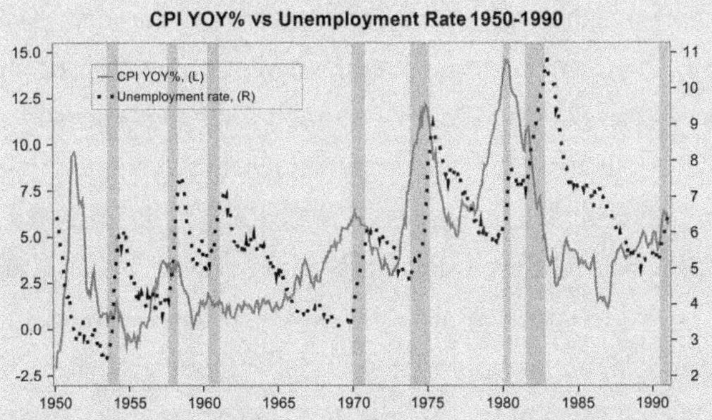

fig 10.7

Source: Macrobond, Mizuho Securities USA, Bloomberg, BLS, US Federal Reserve System

CPI, y-o-y% vs. USA Unemployment Rate, 1950–1990

Unfortunately, the costs associated with the Cold War, the international demand for dollars by recovering Western economies, and the social reforms demanded at home were too much for the system to handle. In relatively short order, the system collapsed. In the post–Bretton Woods fiat money world, inflation initially accelerated, as economists had feared. Within just eight years of President Nixon closing the gold window and ending the dollar/peg system, the dollar was in sharp decline in value and prestige while inflation had morphed into a wage-price spiral and stagflation.

The unexpected outcome of rising inflation and rising

unemployment resulted in fundamental shifts in economic thinking, both about the role of money in the economy as well as the efficacy of fiscal policy. This philosophical shift eventually resulted in today's world of global excess supply of tradable goods and deflationary pressure, despite fiat monetary regimes throughout the developed world. The shift from excess demand to excess supply for goods and services appears to have fundamentally altered the dynamics of the economy and will be discussed more fully in the final section of this book. Before we can begin that discussion, a detailed look at the currency markets, exchange rate determination, and the domestic approach to trade will prove valuable. The declining value of the dollar and its impact on inflation were critical drivers behind the shifts in macro policy of the 1980s that put the economy on the course that brought us to today's uncharted territory.

Section 3

Money's Role Reversal

Chapter 11

The Relative Value of Money

So far, we have looked at the theoretical and practical/historical aspects of money. In particular, we have examined the role money plays in determining real growth and inflation and how economic thinking on these dynamic relationships has evolved since the Great Depression. We reviewed the Keynesian model of the economy in the traditional IS–LM framework. In this model, money is seen as one of the key policy levers that can be manipulated to fine-tune the economy and hopefully eliminate, or at least mute, the business cycle. Policy makers can also directly influence the economy through outright purchases of goods and services and with tax policy/fiscal policy.

All of this lays the groundwork for why money is at the center of macro models designed to determine the equilibrium values for growth and inflation. The transition from Keynes to Friedman and the Chicago school of monetarism that followed was the logical outgrowth of the unanticipated inflationary spiral of the late 1970s and 1980s. The wage-price link and the stagflation that followed led to the belief that, in the long term, money has little, if any, effect on real GDP but is closely correlated with inflation. This decisive shift in thinking, backed up by empirical analysis, led to the Federal Reserve explicitly targeting the supply of money available in the economy, as opposed to its long history of targeting the level of short-term interest rates. This experiment, with targeting money as the main determinant of monetary policy, did not last very long, as financial innovation began to blur the lines between financial liabilities that could be used for transaction purposes and those that represented savings balances. This naturally led to the hybrid policy approach where the Federal Reserve is guided by its mandate to foster sustainable noninflationary, long-term growth where liquidity conditions in the economy are one of the key determinants of monetary policy.

Subsequently, we looked at the practical side of money. What is money? How can it be measured? And we saw different monetary regimes that have been implemented over the course of history, particularly in this country. We discussed the pros and cons of a gold coin standard, a gold exchange standard, a gold peg, and today's fiat monetary system. We also addressed the reasons why each of these different monetary systems failed or were historically abandoned. We looked at different forms that money has taken over the centuries and why precious metals have been the dominant form of currency used as a medium of exchange. The relative availability of gold and its obvious physical qualities explain why it was initially used over silver as a medium of exchange for transactions. As people became adept at extracting all sorts of metal from the earth, various combinations of coins have been minted.

The benefit of a gold coin standard and/or a gold exchange standard is that gold has a value based simply on its physical qualities, whereas paper money derives its value only from the gold that backs it in a gold exchange standard. A principal benefit of a gold standard is that money in this form tends to maintain a fairly stable value, which facilitates transactions not only domestically but also internationally; that is, it eases the process of international trade as the value attached to goods and services can easily be compared across geographic regions. A major limitation of a gold standard is the fixed supply of the metal in the short run, which imposes a constraint on growth. More important, economic imbalances under a gold standard prompt self-correcting flows of the precious metal between economies, which is another important benefit of following a gold standard, but it's also a major detraction. Inflationary pressures and/or trade deficits will automatically lead to an outflow of gold from an economy, reversing these undesired developments, but at the cost of rising interest rates, rising unemployment, and deflationary pressures. This adjustment mechanism and the deflation it induced is one of the key reasons why business cycles prior to World War II tended to be depressions instead of recessions. The adverse effects imposed on the economy due to the limited supply of gold and the forced deflationary pressures triggered by temporary imbalances prompted policy makers to seek an alternative monetary regime that would increase flexibility but still maintain the stability provided by gold.

Bretton Woods was an attempt at creating a "best of all

worlds" monetary environment. The agreement created a gold-peg standard. The dollar was valued in terms of gold, as were all other IMF-participating currencies, but these would also be allowed a modest degree of flexibility relative to the dollar. By holding reserves in the form of either gold or US dollars, this provided the system increased flexibility. Unfortunately, in the rapidly changing postwar environment, the Bretton Woods system proved inadequate to deal with the stresses of excess supply and inflationary pressures generated by a rapidly expanding global economy and intense domestic social pressures. The result was rapid domestic inflation and an outflow of gold that did not result in an offsetting economic consolidation or disinflationary pressures. The growing divergence between the secondary price of gold and its official value eventually forced the closing of the US Treasury's gold window and the technical demise of Bretton Woods. After a brief attempt at reviving the gold peg, a fiat monetary system was adopted and is still in effect. Yet, despite the repeated failure of systems more rigid than the current one, there is still a vocal minority that desires a return to gold. This belief is reflected in the continued safe-haven status of gold and the development of cryptocurrencies, which will be discussed later.

The evolving nature of money, both in theory and in practice, is still an ongoing phenomenon. But before we can fully discuss the conditions that have created this environment, in which an expansive monetary policy can and does coexist with deflationary pressures, a basic understanding of the foreign exchange market and its determinants is necessary, as the value of the currency becomes a key determinant of growth and inflation in a fiat currency world. We will discuss the difference between a fixed versus a floating exchange rate system; the factors that drive foreign exchange trading; and the relative value of money in a fiat currency world.

Fixed vs. Floating

Just as there are two major types of monetary regimes—a commodity/precious metal or a fiat standard—there are also two principal exchange rate systems—fixed or floating. Essentially, a fixed exchange rate system is one in which the government decides the conversion rate. Alternatively, when the exchange rate is determined by market forces, it is called a floating exchange rate. Between these two major systems there are many different variations, such as a crawling peg or a managed float.

A fixed exchange rate is determined by a government or monetary authority and not by market forces. Only small deviations from the official conversion rate are allowed, as central banks stand ready to buy and sell at a fixed price. A fixed exchange rate system is typically associated with a precious metal or gold standard, assuming each currency is defined in terms of gold. As such, the exchange rate or conversion rate between different currencies is fixed in terms of the physical quantity of gold backing the two sides of any given currency pair.

The principal merits of a fixed exchange rate are that it encourages foreign trade, as it reduces risks and uncertainty associated with international transactions. To maintain a fixed exchange system, central banks are required to coordinate macro policy. A fixed exchange rate system ensures that major economic disturbances in member countries are quickly reversed and, as such, it prevents long-term capital outflows. Speculation is also minimized, as investors are forced to confront the combined weight of multiple central banks, coordinating policies. The main flaw in this system is that when problems arise, like sustained periods of excess demand and persistently rising inflation, the risk of large one-off devaluations increases.

A flexible exchange rate system is one in which market forces determine exchange rates. The value of the currency can fluctuate according to the balance between the supply and demand for foreign exchange. Under this system, central banks are not obliged to offset deviations in the currency rates, which means that the market trades freely. A key advantage of this system is that balance of payments surpluses or deficits are automatically corrected. It also helps optimize resource allocations, as currency movements reflect the market's assessment of relative productivity. In addition, a flexible exchange rate system provides some protection from importing overseas inflation and/or deflation pressures, as the currency either appreciates or depreciates accordingly. Monetary policy becomes more effective with a floating exchange rate by stimulating short-term capital flows, which reinforces the effects of interest rates on aggregate demand. This system lowers the need for international reserves, as currencies can freely float. A major demerit of a floating exchange rate system is that it allows potentially destabilizing market speculation. Resource utilization costs are also increased, as capital flows and exchange rate adjustments lead to suboptimal shifting of productive capital. Some would also argue that the dampening of overseas influences on inflation should be considered a negative, because it reduces the need for monetary discipline by the central bank.

Fiat monetary regimes by their nature lend themselves to a floating exchange rate system, but this is not a requirement, as some countries still fix their currencies and have even joined in monetary unions. However, the mix of merits and demerits of these two exchange rate systems makes it difficult to determine which system is superior. Yet, it is clear that a robust foreign market has developed to offset many of the risks associated with today's floating exchange rate system.

TRADE ACCOUNTING

Understanding what is meant by the terms of trade and what trade statistics tell us about the economy is critical to understanding why foreign exchange is key to deciphering the role of money in the economy. The terms of trade, or TOT, is defined as the relative price of exports in terms of imports and is calculated by the ratio of export prices to import prices. This ratio, or TOT, can be interpreted as the amount of imported goods an economy can purchase per unit of exported goods. An improvement in the terms of trade benefits the economy in the sense that more imported goods can be purchased per unit of exports. Changes in the exchange rate clearly can have a big effect on the TOT. Changes in the terms of trade will be reflected in a country's key trade-related statistics. The three most important are: (1) the current account; (2) the capital account; and (3) the balance of payments.

Current Account. A country's current account consists of the balance of trade or net exports, net factor income, or earnings on foreign assets minus payments made to foreign investors, and net cash transfers, which occur over a specific period, typically one quarter. A current account surplus indicates that the value of a country's net foreign assets grew over the quarter or perhaps a year. A current account deficit indicates that a country's net foreign assets shrank over the quarter. Both government and private payments are included in its calculation. A current account surplus indicates that a nation is a net lender to the rest of the world, while a deficit indicates that a nation is a net borrower. A current account surplus can also indicate that a nation's net foreign assets increase by the value of the surplus over one quarter and vice versa for a deficit. In a fixed exchange rate system, a current account surplus or deficit is corrected by the flow of gold between countries and its effect on money, inflation, interest rates, and the pace of economic growth.

In a floating exchange rate regime, a current account deficit must be offset by a surplus in the capital account (discussed below). To reduce a current account deficit, countries typically apply import restrictions, quotas, duties, or promote exports. Exchange rate devaluation is another tool often utilized by the deficit country to try to improve its relative position. Some governments adjust their spending patterns to benefit domestic manufacturers, which can also improve the current account. Moreover, it is called the current account because the goods and services measured are consumed/earned in the current quarter.

Capital Account. The capital account measures the net change in the ownership of national assets. It measures the difference between the change in foreign ownership of domestic assets and the change in domestic ownership of foreign assets. A capital account surplus means money is flowing into a country, while a deficit means money is flowing out. With a surplus, foreigners are increasing their ownership of domestic assets, while a deficit means domestic investors are increasing their ownership of foreign assets. There are four major components of the capital account: (1) net foreign direct investment; (2) net portfolio investment; (3) net other investment; and (4) the net central bank reserve account. Net foreign direct investment refers to long-term capital investment—principally physical investment in plants, real estate, and equipment. Net portfolio investment includes the net purchase of stocks and bonds in the market—these can be either short-term or long-term assets. The other category includes net flows from banks either into or out of account balances or net lending. The final category, the reserve account, represents the net purchase or sale of foreign exchange by the central bank. Under a fixed exchange rate regime like Bretton Woods, countries generally adopt strict capital controls to reduce speculative pressure on the currency peg. Under a fiat/floating rate regime, capital flows are needed to offset current account imbalances and maintain the balance of payments.

Balance of Payments (BOP). The balance of payments is a record of all economic transactions between residents of a country or nation and the rest of the world over a specific period. These transactions are made by individuals, firms, and various government entities. BOP provides detailed information on the demand and supply of a country's currency. The components of the BOP can indicate how other countries view a nation as a potential business partner. Alternatively, the data can indicate a country's net competitive position. Essentially, the BOP keeps a systematic record of all economic transactions with all other countries over a specific period. Due to its double-entry accounting, all receipts from abroad are recorded as credits and all payments overseas are logged as debits. When all components of the BOP are included, they must sum to zero—no surplus or deficit.

If a country is running a current account deficit, then its capital account will have to be in surplus—this capital account surplus can be obtained. Just because the overall BOP needs to net to zero when all items are included, imbalances can occur, and are likely in the individual components. Under a fixed exchange rate system, the central bank tends to be an important player in keeping the BOP at zero, while in a floating rate system, the currency tends to be the key factor keeping the BOP at zero. As such, central bank reserves tend to be a passive component of the BOP.

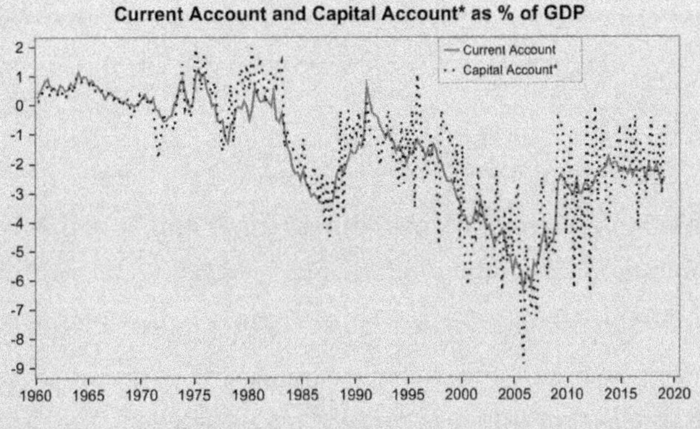

fig 11.1

Source: Macrobond, Mizuho Securities USA, BEA

US Current Account vs. Capital Account

Exchange Rate Market

A floating exchange rate system tends to be associated with a fiat monetary regime, and a robust foreign exchange market helps smooth the transactions process and mitigate risks.

The modern foreign exchange market began to take shape during the 1970s, after the collapse of the Bretton Woods system. The three decades prior were dominated by government restrictions on currency transactions. But after the gold-peg standard failed and countries moved to a floating exchange rate/fiat monetary regime, currency trading became a central pillar of today's highly interconnected global financial markets. Currently, financial transactions dwarf real sector transactions in a world where financial institutions operate in many regions and across multiple time zones. In fact, bank-related markets, of which foreign exchange is the largest, trade around the clock.

Several unique aspects of the exchange marketplace are at the center of a rapidly expanding global marketplace, not just for commodities and manufactured goods, but also for financial services. One thing that makes this market unique is its size. The market for foreign exchange is the largest of all, with an estimated $6 trillion a day in daily volume when it peaked in 2014. Because most countries have their own currency, currency trading is spread across the globe, with London, New York, and Tokyo serving as regional trading centers for around-the-clock trading. This highly efficient and liquid marketplace ensures tight bid/ask spreads and thin margins.

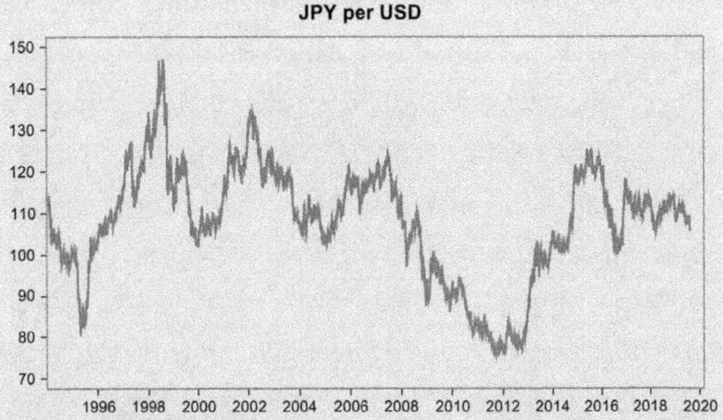

***fig* 11.2**

Source: Macrobond, Mizuho Securities USA, Bloomberg, IMF

Pound/$ Rate

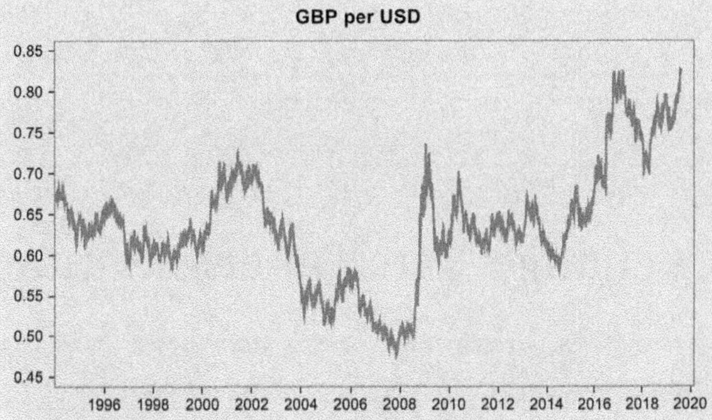

***fig* 11.3**

Source: Macrobond, Mizuho Securities USA, Bloomberg, IMF

Yen/$

Because countries generally defend the value of their currencies, leverage is also a big component of this market. The foreign exchange market ballooned after Bretton Woods' collapse, and the need to hedge exchange rate risk resulted in the rapid growth of new products, which include forwards, swaps, options, and futures. This suite of derivative products, tied to spot currency trading, greatly expanded the scope of transactions trading and hedging, as well as reducing the cost of speculative trading. The fact that a fiat currency's value is dependent on a variety of factors is another important driver behind the growth in foreign exchange trading in comparison to the pure transactional environment that existed under a gold standard. The spot foreign exchange rate reflects the relative value of a currency, not its absolute value, as currencies trade in pairs, one against the other or on the cross. As such, the key drivers of currency trading and exchange rates can shift, based on evolving economic conditions.

Exchange Rate Determination

Money is seen as a claim on a society's future worth under a fiat currency model. This implies that exchange rates reflect the investment communities' relative assessment of the expected future difference between two countries' expected value. Essentially, a rising exchange rate suggests that the expected future value of the country whose currency is appreciating is rising relative to that of the base currency in the currency pair.

For example, if the yen rises relative to the dollar, then the expected future worth of Japan is seen as improving relative to that of the United States. The expected future value of a society is a very complex calculation, and over time, the relative weights of the factors that feed into this analysis may shift with changing social and geopolitical trends. As such, forecasting exchange rates is more difficult than forecasting an economy's growth potential, its inflation, and the structure of interest rates because you also need to forecast the relative position of a host of different countries in the future. Also, their relative political stability and geopolitical standing, as seen by different societies, is reflected in investment preferences.

The ever-changing dynamics of what drivers determine exchange rates can be seen in the roller-coaster ride the dollar has taken since the 1970s. Shortly after the end of Bretton Woods, and the shift to a freely floating US dollar, the exchange rate came under downward pressure as inflation spiked during the late 1970s and early 1980s. The so-called wage/price spiral caused a radical rethink of monetary policy by the Fed. The shift from the Keynesian macro model to the Friedman-Schwartz monetarist model resulted in a spike in short-term interest rates and a sharp reversal in the dollar. Instead of a declining exchange rate, the Fed's anti-inflation push resulted in a dramatic appreciation of the dollar. As the dollar surged, the US trade deficit began to swell, and the deficit exploded in the wake of the Reagan supply-side tax cut. Eventually, concerns over the ballooning twin trade deficits weakened the dollar. This protracted weakening of the dollar reversed in the wake of the disinflationary trend that materialized in the 1990s. The shift away from traditional manufacturing toward the rapidly evolving technology industry in the United States caused a flood of global investors' money into the emerging technology companies that would soon become household words, like Intel, Cisco, AOL, and JDS.

The rush to be part of the new digital age pushed the dollar back upward as the economy accelerated and equity markets pushed to new highs. The resulting explosion in tax revenue reversed the deteriorating trend in the budget deficit, resulting in investors' concern over the pending scarcity of Treasury notes and bonds that pulled long-term yields lower as inflation continued to drift unexpectedly lower. The Clinton equity market rally was turbocharged by the dot-com craze, and the speculative flows into the equity market pushed the dollar higher. When the dot-com bubble burst, the dollar began a long slide that continued right until the financial crisis erupted in 2007. During the six-year expansion, between 2001 and 2007, the dollar declined despite a renewed equity market rally and a powerful rebound in the economy, as the construction industry benefited from lower long-term rates. The weakness in the dollar over this period was generally the result of the lost international prestige associated with the second Gulf War, the Bush administration's deemphasizing the Clinton's strong dollar policy, and the Fed's decision not to prick the real estate bubble with higher rates as it inflated. Eventually, the housing bubble burst, as all speculative crazes eventually do, and the resulting global financial crisis led to a rebound in the dollar. The dollar's brief appreciation during the Great Recession was the result of the Fed's leadership in cleaning up the financial mess created by the bursting of the housing bubble.

A combination of zero short-term interest rates and a host of nontraditional policy initiatives, along with the government's rescue of AIG and a series of forced banking system mergers, set the stage for the domestic economy to return to growth before the global downturn bottomed. As the rest of the world recovered, and China defied all odds and weathered the global financial crises without sliding into recession, the dollar lost its upside bias and dropped back to its pre-crises low. With Europe and Asia in recovery, the dollar drifted a bit lower. But when the Fed decided to end its accommodative policies and began hiking rates, the dollar firmed again, and it has generally trended sideways into mid-2019. These shifts in the dollar reflect the ever-changing drivers of exchange rates, but what is clear is that we can isolate several macroeconomic factors that have proven to be important in determining the dollar's exchange rate over the last fifty years:

1. *Inflation Rates.* According to the purchasing power parity model, relative inflation is a key determinant of the exchange rate. The country with the lowest rate of inflation should have the strongest currency, while the country with the highest rate of inflation should have the weakest currency. Deflation reverses things, in that the country with the highest rate of deflation is the strongest of the currency pair.
2. *Interest Rates.* Changes in interest rates affect a currency's value. Specifically, exchange rates, interest rates, and

inflation are all correlated. An increase in interest rates causes a country's currency to appreciate if the relative increase in rates attracts a greater share of investable funds.

3. *Current Account/Balance of Payments.* The current account reflects the balance of trade and earnings on foreign investments. A deficit in the current account due to spending more on imports than earned on exports causes the country's currency value to depreciate.
4. *Government Debt.* The higher the level of government debt outstanding, the higher the necessary real rate is to attract investors. This implies that the greater the deficit, the weaker the currency, on a relative basis.
5. *Terms of Trade.* The higher the ratio of export to import prices, the more favorable the terms of trade, and the more net revenue domestic companies will earn. This implies a greater demand for the currency and that the terms of trade have improved—leading to a firming in the exchange rate.
6. *Political Stability and Performance.* A country's political situation can affect its currency's strength. A country with less political turmoil and a more constructive approach to business will tend to have a stronger currency. Specifically, a country with sound financial and trade policies will see its currency benefit.
7. *Speculation.* Investors' expectation can influence exchange rates and, in the short run, could easily be more important than any of the other more macro variables listed above—especially in a fiat model, where policy officials tend to treat the currency with benign neglect.

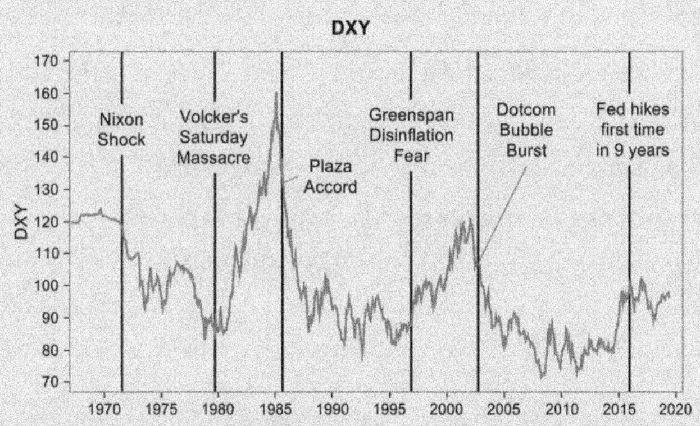

***fig* 11.4**

Source: Macrobond, Mizuho Securities USA, Bloomberg

Trade-Weighted Dollar Index

The above factors have been well-documented drivers of exchange rate fluctuations since the early 1970s. Modeling the dollar, however, has proven very difficult due to the apparent random nature of the shifts in the factors determining the dollar's relative value. But one important trend that has emerged is the amplitude of the shift in the exchange rate, which has diminished over time after initially spiking following the transition to a fiat system. This trend toward moderation in the exchange rate probably reflects the fact that since the late 1980s inflation has become less volatile as well. This supports our contention that, at the end of the day, purchasing-power parity is at the core of currency valuation.

The dampening in inflation is the result of a confluence of factors that will be discussed later, when we evaluate the effects of the transition to a fiat model for money. Before we get into this topic, and how it plays into the recent interests in cryptocurrencies, Modern Monetary Theory, and the search for alternative macro policy levers, a historical perspective on US trade policy will be useful, since the drive for free trade has been one of the key factors credited for having dampened inflation pressures domestically and globally.

A Long History of Protectionist Leanings

The exchange rate systems discussed earlier in this chapter, and the different monetary regimes that enabled their development, all have two things in common: (1) the desire of policy makers to expand foreign trade between countries by establishing a stable exchange rate environment; and (2) allowing enough flexibility in money supply so that liquidity issues no longer hinder economic growth in the face of imbalances.

Under a precious metal standard or any other commodity-based monetary system, the exchange rate tends to be fixed by the relative weight of the commodity backing each currency in a relative pair. The exchange rate system shifts to a floating rate structure in a fiat monetary model. With a fixed exchange rate, the currency's volatility is clearly not a limitation on foreign trade. Currency volatility definitely becomes more of an issue when money is unhinged from precious metals and is defined as a future claim on a society's worth.

During the period when the dollar was explicitly tied to gold, the United States established considerably high tariffs in order to protect domestic industries. Alternatively, the push toward more open trade began in this country after President Roosevelt ended the classic gold standard and moved the country to a gold exchange standard. The next big step occurred in the mid-to-late 1970s, when President Nixon closed the gold window, moving the dollar to a fiat standard. We will see later that the push toward free trade has played a critical role in the transition from excess demand to excess supply, and the fact that excessive money growth has not led to inflation and devaluation in the currency since the 2007–2008 financial crisis. The history and motivation behind the evolution of trade practices in the United States will help set the stage for our later discussion of how the transition to excess supply evolved in the post-1990s period.

The history of tariffs in this country can be traced back to the nation's beginnings. To pay off the debt accumulated during the Revolutionary War, Congress passed the Tariff Act of 1789 as its second official act. This imposed a 5 percent tariff on nearly all imports. The argument advanced by Alexander Hamilton in favor of the tariff was that there was a need to protect "infant industries and workers" in this country from cheaper, more established overseas exporters. The need to develop a domestic defense industry and self-sufficiency was another reason behind the desire to nurture domestic industries. Between 1792 and the War of 1812, the average tariff level increased to 12.5 percent, then increased further to 25 percent to defer the cost of the war. By 1816, import tariffs were raised again to 35 percent, as industrialists lobbied to further protect their competitive position. The workers seeing the benefits of these tariffs supported a hike to 40 percent in 1820.

Although tariff policies were not a major motivation for the Civil War, there was a clear difference of opinion on this topic between the industrialists in the North, who favored high tariffs, and the agricultural South, which supported lower tariffs. Once the war erupted, the South's need for revenue led to the Confederacy also imposing high tariffs. After the war and through Reconstruction, voters generally viewed tariffs as favorable, and as a result, additional increases were undertaken. By 1875, as Reconstruction neared its end, tariffs on imported manufactured goods ranged from 40 percent to 50 percent. European policy makers, in contrast, pursued very different paths during this period, seeing tariffs as a drag on the economy. This divergence resulted in European tariffs of only 9 percent to 12 percent.

Support for tariff protection continued through the period of domestic industrialization, but opposition was beginning to be organized against the higher cost associated with the established system of domestic subsidy. As domestic manufacturers overtook their European counterparts in productivity, size, and profitability, support for high protective tariffs began to wane. But entrenched political interests remained in control of the debate until 1909, when the Payne-Aldrich Tariff Act lowered tariffs on Midwest farm products while raising them on industrial products. The outbreak of World War I in 1914 again forced an increase in tariffs, even though the income tax that began back in 1861 was now the primary source of revenue for the government.

The next big increase in tariffs occurred just around the time the Depression began, when Congress passed the Smoot-Hawley Tariff Act in 1930. This legislation increased tariffs on over 20,000 imported goods and resulted in the second-highest tariff rate in 100 years. According to the US Census Bureau, the average tariff on goods covered by the legislation increased from 40.1 percent in 1929 to 59.1 percent in 1932. This legislation and the retaliatory actions taken by foreign governments are considered important contributors to the global collapse in exports that exacerbated the Depression.

Shift Toward Open Markets

The Depression changed the tariff debate as much as Roosevelt's New Deal shifted the approach of the federal government to a progressive agenda. Congress passed the Reciprocal Tariff Act in 1934, authorizing the president to negotiate a bilateral tariff reduction with other countries, sidestepping the long, drawn-out, and politically contentious process driven by Congress. The shift in thinking regarding the benefits of open markets suggested that expanding trade would help stimulate growth. However, no one country wanted to unilaterally cut tariffs and take the chance that others would follow. As a result, between 1934 and 1945, the executive branch negotiated more than thirty-two bilateral trade liberalization deals with other countries. The shift toward internationalism from the protectionist ways that dominated from the Revolutionary War to the end of World War II appears to have been motivated more by ideas of exploiting America's unique economic position after the war than by a true shift in ideology. The benefits of an open market were perceived to be more favorable than continuing to pursue protectionist tendencies.

Trade liberalization accelerated following World War II, as the United States promoted the General Agreement on Tariffs and Trade (GATT), which was established in 1947 to reduce tariffs and other impediments to trade. GATT became the World Trade Organization (WTO) in 1995 with the end of the Cold War, and open markets and low-tariff ideology became the dominant economic model. The North American Free Trade Act (NAFTA) is probably the peak of the free trade era in the United States. This agreement was signed by President Clinton and came into effect on January 1, 1994. Notably, this piece of legislation was initiated by President Reagan in 1980 but took fourteen years to bring to fruition. The initial agreement eliminated or reduced a host of obstacles to trade and capital flows between the United States, Canada, and Mexico. At the insistence of President Trump, this agreement was renegotiated, and is still awaiting ratification by all its members.

The push toward free trade between 1947 and 2018 was not without setbacks. For example, the domestic auto industry lobbied for protection in the early 1980s, resulting in voluntary import restrictions being negotiated with Japan. This three-year voluntary limit on Japanese cars exported into this country had the same effect as an increase in tariffs, without the requirement of higher tariffs or formal legislation. This program was extended repeatedly and was eventually removed in 1994, ten years after its original expiration. Other more modest disputes occurred during this 72-year period, but none was as politically charged as the 25 percent tax on all imported light trucks imposed by President Johnson in 1964. This tax was in response to West Germany having imposed restrictive tariffs on poultry imports to protect local farmers.

Rethinking the Benefits of Free Trade and Other Long-Held Macro Doctrines

The seventy-year push opening markets and expanding global trade that was experienced at the end of World War I appears to have somewhat run its course. President Trump's decision to pull out of the Trans-Pacific Partnership in 2017 was a major setback for the free trade initiative. His insistence on renegotiating NAFTA is another sign that the view toward trade is changing. The administration asserts that it is pro free trade and that it is only anti-large multilateral deals that diminish the bargaining power of the United States, yet little progress on the planned bilateral deals is evident. Instead, the administration appears to have begun using trade as a weapon to achieve geopolitical objectives. The trade war with China begun by the administration is a clear attempt to use economic leverage to further democratic ideals where open markets and economic growth failed.

It is interesting that the pushback on free trade has evolved against the backdrop of the 2007 financial crisis, or the so-called Great Recession. The shift toward internationalism was, coincidently, a direct response to the Great Depression and the war that followed. This rethink on free trade stems from the deteriorating current account deficit experienced since the 1970s and the growing belief that overseas markets are not as open to exports as domestic markets are to imports. This has led to calls for a more level playing field, or fair trade, instead of free trade. The shallow growth trajectory that has followed the deep and protracted 2007–2009 recession has clearly been a further source of frustration, with the evolution of the postwar economic environment. In addition, deflationary trends that evolved over the ten years since the recession ended have caused policy makers to question their models and the value of policy tools that have been relied upon for generations.

The deflation bias is perhaps the most unsettling of all the post-crises developments, as it has coincided with a significant expansion in the Federal Reserve's balance sheet. The monetization of the debt was long feared as the ultimate debasement of the currency; yet none of the dreaded inflationary consequences have materialized. The lack of domestic inflation pressure is even more surprising than the deflation pressures in

Europe and Japan, despite the balance-sheet expansion undertaken by the Bank of Japan and the European Central Bank. The domestic economy is clearly running with a much higher level of resource utilization than the other advanced economies. This means either the role of money in the economy (as discussed in Sections 1 and 2 of this book) has changed or there is something more powerful than money affecting the economy domestically and internationally.

We devote the rest of this analysis to interpreting the events that have transpired since President Nixon took the country off the gold standard, and how these developments have shifted the global economy from a world of excess demand to that of excess supply. This shift has altered the way economists and policy makers need to think about the role of money and the broader macroeconomic dynamic.

Chapter 12

Worst Fears Realized

The dramatic breakdown of the Bretton Woods system and the shift to a fiat monetary regime was triggered by a run on US gold reserves in the late 1960s. This run was caused by foreign central banks that grew increasingly worried about the acceleration in inflation gripping this country. After a string of failed attempts by governments to rescue the system, continued imbalances in trade flows and accelerating domestic inflation forced President Nixon to abruptly close the gold window on August 15, 1971. This radical step was a key component of the administration's emergency program to wring inflation out of the economy and rebuild global confidence in the value of the US dollar. The 1971 initiative also included a freeze on wages and prices as well as a surcharge on imported oil. In retrospect, the decision to end international convertibility of the dollar looks like a natural solution to the drain on US Treasury gold reserves and the other accumulating problems plaguing the international monetary system. But at the time, this was a very controversial move by the administration.

Although the United States had adopted a fiat standard

a couple of times before in its history, the fact that none of these monetary experiments turned out well added to the concerns that surrounded the president's unorthodox decision. Additionally, the memory of the demise of the Weimar Republic and its citizens going shopping with wheelbarrows full of worthless marks was still fresh in the minds of policy makers. The financial collapse of the post–World War I German republic is credited with setting the stage for the rise of extremism that embroiled Europe in a second war just two decades later. These historical lessons added additional uncertainty to the Nixon decision. The dollar's central role as the world's reserve currency, moreover, added to the trepidation of the policy makers who would ultimately be held responsible for unhinging the dollar from gold.

Cracks in the Foundation

It is interesting to note that the inflation pressures of the 1960s would lead to the demise of Bretton Woods, because it was the discipline of gold that was supposed to keep the dollar's value steady and inflation under control in the postwar financial system envisioned by Harry White, its principal architect. Unfortunately, the system adopted at Bretton Woods required the Federal Reserve, at times, to subordinate domestic monetary policy needs in favor of international demands on policy. This aspect of the system proved to be its fatal flaw, especially with the Keynesian monetary policy approach being followed by the Fed. This approach implied that the Fed was responsible for setting the level of short-term rates to support the fiscal policy priorities of elected officials.

The resulting conflict of interest emerged very early on in the Bretton Woods period, as the Johnson administration pushed the twin policy initiatives of expanding the social contract domestically, while escalating the US military involvement in the Vietnam War. The "Great Society" experiment included not only the Civil Rights Act of 1964 and the Voting Rights Act of 1965, but it also included the War on Poverty initiative, the Elementary and Secondary Education Act of 1965, and the creation of several new entitlements. Medicare, Medicaid, and welfare were all authorized as part of the Social Security Act of 1965 sponsored by the administration.

The costs of these new programs were added on top of the boost to the economy created by the Kennedy tax cut, or the Revenue Tax Act of 1964, that was signed into law by President Johnson early that year. The main provisions of this legislation were to cut the top marginal tax rate for individuals to 70 percent from 91 percent and to cut 4 percent in corporate taxes, to 44 percent from 48 percent. The additional cost of the Johnson social programs was huge. In 1962, before this social experiment began, the mandatory portion of total government spending was about 30 percent of the budget; within a short period, that share had grown to more than 60 percent of total government outlays.

The escalation of the Vietnam War was another big infusion of stimulus to the economy. It has been estimated that the cost of the war effort, in today's dollars, would be upwards of $1 trillion in spending on equipment and logistical support for a total of 2.6 million servicemen and women who served in the conflict. This includes the cost of munitions dropped by B-52s, the artillery shells expended, the 4,900 helicopters, and the 3,700 jets used over the fourteen years of the conflict. The stimulus provided by these initiatives was in addition to the spending associated with both the arms and space races that epitomized the Cold War period, especially during the 1960s.

Resource utilization rose decidedly after the relatively long ten-month recession that began in April 1960 and bottomed in February 1961, as the economy benefited from the Fed having taken its foot off the monetary brakes and as these new government programs began to kick in. Over the course of the ensuing expansion, the jobless rate plunged from over 7 percent to below 3.5 percent, as the economy moved well into what would become a 106-month expansion. The 1960s expansion would turn out to be one of the more robust upturns, as the growing middle class flexed its economic muscle.

Fed policymakers supported this expansion, consistent with the Keynesian model, allowing the growth in money supply to accelerate to a little more than 7.5 percent, from a low of about 1.5 percent, over the course of the 1960s expansion. The result was a rapid shift in the economy, from running well below capacity to stretching the economy's constraints to the extent that it had only previously experienced during the war. Headline inflation in the 1960s, as a result, accelerated to more than 3.5 percent from a benign 1 percent rate, and the dollar began to weaken. Gold prices also began to climb relative to the official price of $35 an ounce. Besides the deterioration in domestic inflation and the downward pressure this exerted on the dollar, the US share of global GDP dropped sharply between 1950 and 1969, to 27 percent from 39 percent, as Europe and Asia recovered from the war. This combination of shifting fundamentals put upward pressure on the market price for gold, eventually eroding the willingness of central banks to hold dollars and defend the official gold price, as called for under the postwar monetary system.

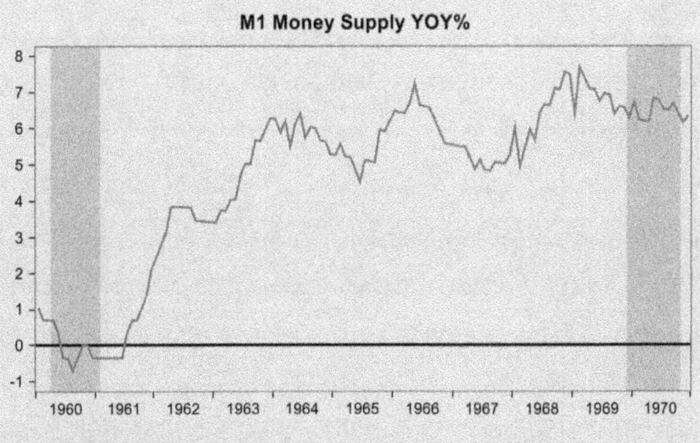

***fig* 12.1**

Source: Macrobond, Mizuho Securities USA, Bloomberg, US Federal Reserve System

Money Supply (MI Growth, 1960 to 1970)

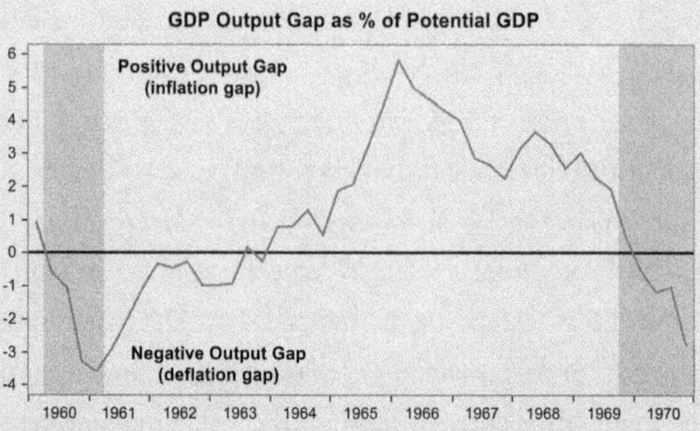

fig **12.2**

Source: Macrobond, Mizuho Securities USA, Bloomberg, CBO, BEA

GDP Output Gap, 1960 to 1970

The growing divergence between the official dollar conversion price set by Bretton Woods and market prices further incentivized foreign central banks to convert their excess dollar holdings into gold to protect the value of their reserves. Meanwhile, the drain on US gold reserves began to be an issue for the Treasury. This divergence widened to over $7 an ounce in 1968, following the collapse of the London Gold Pool (discussed in Chapter 9), showing the degree to which confidence and the fundamentals skewed away from the dollar. The stress on the dollar continued to build, as did the run on the US Treasury's gold reserves, and by 1971, when the gold window was closed, the market price for gold climbed. At one point, it was $9 higher than the level set by President Nixon that year. One year later, the market price for gold had surged more than $20 an ounce, to $65.20.

Bad Only Got Worse

The situation only got worse once the dollar was no longer converted into gold, which is exactly what policy makers feared. Their concern at the time of the Bretton Woods conference (July 1944) was that unless the new global monetary system was linked to gold, the tendency for governments to inflate their way out of their debts would be a major financial impediment to sustained growth and rising prosperity. The ability to inflate money supply would be overwhelming for policy makers in the new republics of Europe and Asia, as the short-term benefits would clearly outweigh the long-term cost of monetizing the debt.

Little did Harry Dexter White and his boss, Treasury Secretary Henry Morgenthau Jr., realize that it would be imbalances in the US economy, not overseas, that would bring about the inflationary pressures that killed the system they designed. The demise of the postwar dollar peg system, in fact, led to a wage/price spiral, a collapse in the value of the dollar, and a dramatic shift in the thrust of both domestic monetary and fiscal policy. The late 1970s and early 1980s were marked by spikes in inflation, combined with a rising jobless rate—a previously unanticipated economic environment. This politically unacceptable situation would come to be known as stagflation. This worst-of-all-worlds development would force a radical rethink of how the economy functions and how policy makers are supposed to manage the economy to achieve long-term sustainable growth.

The confluence of factors that created the stagflation of the late 1970s and early 1980s was varied and deeply embedded in the economy; it would only be rooted out by a radical shift in policy orchestrated by President Reagan and Paul Volcker, the chairman of the Federal Reserve Board of Governors. At the heart of stagflation was an inflationary psychology that became deeply rooted in household expectations and corporate culture. The belief that prices would continue to accelerate prompted the introduction of Cost of Living Adjustments (COLAs) in most union labor agreements negotiated in the 1970s. The COLA link to stagflation is important since it breaks the weakened relationship between wages and labor market conditions and adds additional rigidities into the labor market. Inflation's erosion of purchasing power was also becoming a political issue as far back as the late 1960s. Its corrosive effect on society resulted in a COLA provision being included in the 1972 Social Security Amendments. The automatic COLA adjustments became effective in January 1975 and would prove to become the model for similar provisions demanded by unionized labor in the collective bargaining process.

As organized labor unions aimed to safeguard the gains made by workers in the decade immediately after the Vietnam War, and pushed to gain additional benefits like health insurance and improved workplace conditions, companies faced increased costs at the same time that environmental regulations were changing the production process. To stay ahead of these rising costs, companies steadily raised prices, passing these costs on to the consumer, and an adverse feedback loop between wages and prices was established. The excess demand of the postwar period was another key factor that enabled the wage-price spiral to develop.

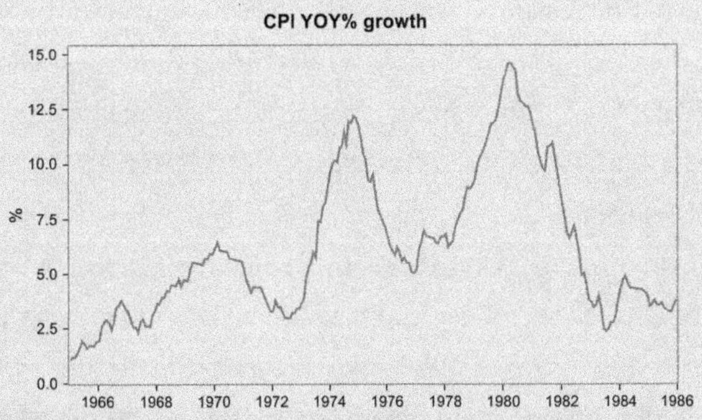

***fig* 12.3**

Source: Macrobond, Mizuho Securities USA, Bloomberg, BLS

CPI Year-Over-Year, 1965 to 1985

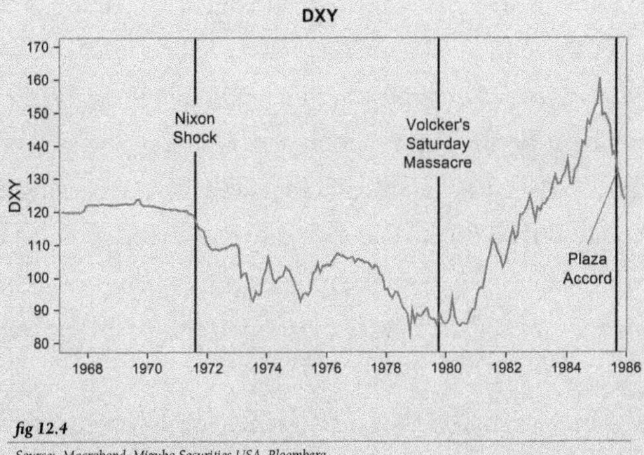

***fig* 12.4**

Source: Macrobond, Mizuho Securities USA, Bloomberg

Trade-Weighted Dollar, 1965 to 1985

Making matters worse was the oil embargo by the Organization of Arab Petroleum Exporting Countries following the 1973 Yom Kippur War. The oil-producing nations in the Mideast imposed the embargo on oil exports and initially targeted Canada, Japan, the Netherlands, the United Kingdom, and the United States for perceived support of Israel during the nineteen-day conflict. The oil export embargo was imposed in October 1973 and was quickly reflected in the price of crude oil and refined product prices. By the end of the embargo in March 1974, the price of crude had risen 400 percent, to nearly $12 a barrel from $3 a barrel. This oil price shock caused major domestic disruptions, as supplies had to be rationed and the increased cost of fuel made a significant share of the US capital stock unproductive, dampening growth and boosting joblessness. The spike in crude and refined product prices was also quickly reflected in consumer inflation, which spiked to over 12 percent from about 2.5 percent, before settling back toward the 5 percent area. The lagged effects of the COLAs pushed up labor costs for companies, squeezing profitability and adding to latent pricing pressure accumulating in the economy, even though crude oil prices stabilized after the embargo was lifted, leaving inflation in the 5 percent area, or twice its pre–oil shock rate.

The November 1973 to March 1975 recession was sixteen months long and resulted in a spike in the civilian jobless rate to its highest rate since the Great Depression. The jobless rate ratcheted upward during the recession, peaking near 9 percent, or approximately 6 percent higher than its previous trough. The Fed's rate hikes were the principal driver of the recession; and even though money growth decelerated significantly as a result of the Fed's tightening, the adjustment in inflation and joblessness in the wake of the eventual easing did not lead to the improvement typically experienced. Both jobless and inflation rates declined in the recessionary period, but to levels well above those expected after previous recessions.

This situation deteriorated even further in the wake of the second oil price shock associated with the Iran hostage crisis that began on November 4, 1979, and did not end until January 20, 1980. During the 444 days of the crisis, incited by the Iranian Revolution, crude oil production was severely constrained by the shift in control from a civilian-led to a cleric-led government. Despite global crude oil production declining by just 4 percent, the price of crude oil more than doubled to over $39 a barrel over the next twelve months, again causing long lines at domestic gasoline service stations.

Fearing its Shi'ite majority would be emboldened by the Iranian Revolution, the Ba'athist government in Iraq, led by Saddam Hussein, initiated the 1980 war with Iran that subsequently crippled oil production in both countries. This reduction in supply caused energy prices to spiral upward, again leading to a spike in consumer prices. This eventually pushed the headline inflation rate toward 15 percent before peaking and beginning a long decline back to the 5 percent area. The spike in inflation was met with a decisive monetary policy response and back-to-back recessions in 1980 and 1981. The combined length of the two recessions was twenty-two months, making it the longest and deepest contraction since the Great Depression. The civilian jobless rate peaked at over 10 percent and the degree of excess capacity generated by the downturn was more than 7 percent of potential real GDP. It was deeper in magnitude than the economic meltdown that followed the financial crises in 2007, according to our calculations, utilizing Congressional Budget Office data for potential GDP.

Stretched to the Breaking Point

The wage-price spiral and the stagflation that gripped the economy in the late 1970s stressed the dollar and the global financial system to its breaking point. The dollar was rapidly losing its value, and global central banks were becoming increasingly reluctant to accumulate dollar-based reserves. The associated increase in financing costs to the US Treasury was limiting the government's ability to tackle problems brought about by sudden and steep erosion in household purchasing power. This situation reached a critical juncture during the early fall of 1979, when Federal Reserve Chairman Paul Volcker announced a radical shift in the focus of domestic monetary policy in order to wring inflation and inflation expectations out of the economy.

Following a rare, unscheduled meeting of the Federal Open Market Committee (FOMC) on Saturday, October 6,

1979, the chairman announced new anti-inflation measures adopted by the committee earlier that day. The chairman had alluded to this new thrust of policy during his confirmation hearing that July. In response to questions from senators during the hearing, Volcker made it clear that the "Fed will have to call the shots as they see them" and that money supply was "rising at a pretty good clip." He further stressed in his remarks that there was no evidence the economy was suffering from a shortage of money. As inflation continued to deteriorate through the summer months and in the wake of growing pressure from other central bankers to take drastic action, the chairman announced that the FOMC would no longer target interest rates. Instead, the Fed would focus its energy on slowing the rate of growth of money. By slowly bringing down the pace of money supply growth, the Fed expected inflation to slow. This shift in policy reflected a fundamental shift in the economic literature away from Keynesianism toward monetarism. This alternative macroeconomic theory (discussed in detail in Chapter 4) postulates that money supply growth has not only a transitory effect on real growth but a permanent effect on inflation. Essentially, the monetarists claim that inflation is a monetary phenomenon, or too much money chasing too few goods and services.

To slow the rate of growth of money to that which is consistent with a sustainable rate of inflation, the Fed would target nonborrowed bank reserves through its open market operations as an intermediate policy target. Focusing on bank reserves as a means of slowing the growth of money, the Fed would allow the interaction between the demand for and the supply of reserves to determine the level of short-term rates in the economy. The results of this new operating procedure were a dramatic rise in the federal funds rate, or the interest rate banks charge for lending reserves to other banks on an overnight unsecured basis. Under the Fed's previous operating procedure, the funds rate was the central bank's principal target. Due to the politically sensitive nature of changing the target rate, policy decisions tended to be slow, allowing inflation imbalances to accumulate. In a world of excess demand, like that experienced early in the postwar period, interest rates below those consistent with sustainable growth quickly led to accelerating inflation.

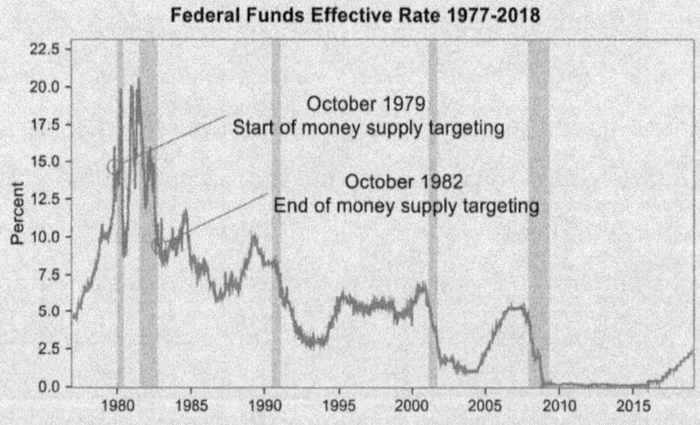

fig 12.5

Source: Macrobond, Mizuho Securities USA, Bloomberg, Federal Reserve Bank of New York

Fed Funds Rate

By breaking the link between policy and the Fed funds rate, political cover was suddenly provided to the Fed, allowing short-term rates to rise to levels previously unacceptable. The Fed funds rate, in fact, climbed to over 22 percent in July 1981, from an average of about 5 percent experienced between 1975 and 1977. The funds rate climbed steadily to 10 percent from 5 percent between 1977 and 1979 as stagflation began to emerge and policy makers struggled with how to address this new dynamic in a Keynesian framework. Following the shift of targeting money supply, the funds rate spiked to over 17 percent before plunging back toward 10 percent as the economy crashed in the wake of the imposition of credit control by the Carter administration. The collapse in economic activity that followed was so severe that policy was quickly reversed, and the Fed went immediately back into tightening mode as the short credit control-induced recession failed to ease inflation pressures. As money growth proved to be much more resilient than expected, short rates kept climbing as the Fed struggled to slow the growth of the monetary aggregates. Besides the economy being pushed back into a deep recession in July 1981 by the extent of the Fed's tightening, the spike in short-term interest rates accelerated the pace of financial engineering, which hastened the end of the Fed's money supply targeting experiment.

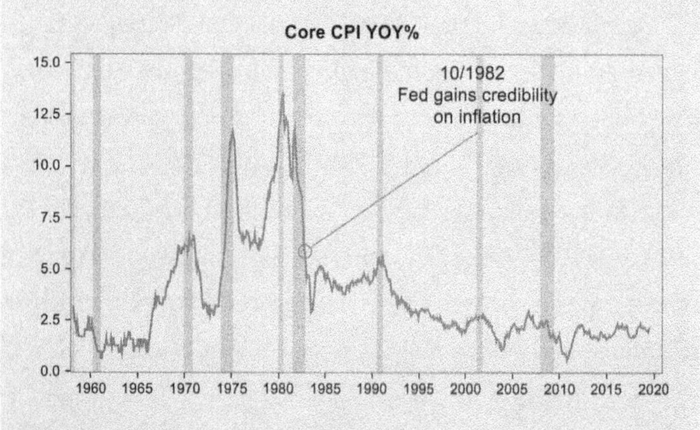

fig **12.6**

Source: Macrobond, Mizuho Securities USA, Bloomberg, BLS

Central Bank Credibility on Inflation

Financial innovation stimulated by excessively high short rates created a host of near money liabilities that subsequently weakened the correlation between money growth and inflation, to the point that just fifteen years after it began targeting the monetary aggregates, the FOMC shifted back to targeting short-term rates. This time, however, the Fed's increased inflation-fighting credibility provided the central bank with enough leeway to increase rates as necessary to keep inflation and inflation expectations well anchored. The fact that many other central banks began adopting an explicit inflation target at this time added intellectual support for the Fed's position that the best way to maximize employment over time and increase the welfare of the country was, and still is, by keeping the inflation genie bottled up at all costs. This new approach has generally been in place since October 1981 and has morphed into a policy of using the level of short-term rates to balance the risks surrounding the outlook for real growth and inflation to achieve the Fed's dual mandate.

It is interesting that the current monetary policy model that has been associated with reduced volatility in the Fed funds rate, over time, has coincided with a decided slowing in the inflation rate. Since 1982, economists and policy makers credit this downshift in inflation to central banks' increased credibility with controlling inflation. This thesis is the generally accepted interpretation of how a fiat monetary standard and a stable inflation rate have come to coexist, despite the risk of the central bank's debt monetization. The spike in inflation that followed in the wake of President Nixon closing the gold window in 1971 was more in line with the worst fears expected by policy makers at the Bretton Woods conference.

Although the central bank's credibility explanation of why inflation became well anchored following the Volcker shift in policy makes for a nice story, it ignores the important fundamental changes in the economy that transpired in the 1980s and 1990s. These changes altered the dynamics of the economy toward a more benign inflation environment. More recently, the shift from excess demand to excess supply has increased the risk of global deflation, even as the Bank of Japan has been in the process of monetizing its debt since the 1990s. Many other regions, including the United States, have followed suit since the financial crisis in 2007.

Central Bank Credibility?

The dramatic decline in inflation that followed the deep, protracted July 1981–November 1982 recession has generally been credited with the aggressive action taken by central banks—in particular, the Federal Reserve—to break the back of the inflation spiral. By implementing a monetarist approach to policy and letting the short rate spike above 22 percent, the Fed earned the respect of market participants for their efforts to rein in inflation. But there is more to this reversal in inflation and inflation expectations than just the central bank's behavior. In general, a fundamental shift in the economy from a position of excess demand to that of excess supply was the critical factor leading to a declaration in inflation, as the central bank's credibility cannot explain the deflation risks evident in the global economy and/or the Fed's desire to try to immunize the domestic economy from these pressures.

Our analysis suggests that the central bank's credibility was clearly an important factor in the initial slide in inflation from its peak of almost 15 percent, but so was the dramatic deterioration in the economy and the excess capacity generated by back-to-back recessions lasting almost two years. This contraction in the economy pushed the output gap to almost 7.5 percent of potential GDP, and the jobless rate up to a high of 10.8 percent in December 1982. Although these cyclical anti-inflation developments clearly played an important role in altering the inflation psychology at the time, the Fed's aggressive move to preemptively hike rates in 1984, just as the recovery/expansion was finding its footing, was clearly a sign that monetary policy now took its inflation-fighting credibility seriously. In fact, the Fed pushed short-term rates back toward 11 percent in its effort to contain any latent inflation pressures in the economy.

The result of this new preemptive inflation-fighting policy was a very shallow rise in inflation, instead of the resumption of a wage-price spiral that had been feared. This moderate upturn in inflation was then quickly followed by a dip into low-single-digit CPI growth, as oil prices collapsed by 40 percent. Increased conservation measures and more energy-efficient technologies that were implemented following the twin energy crises of the 1970s led to this unexpected collapse in energy prices. These efficiencies accumulated over time, and gradually, energy supply began to outstrip demand. This shift in the balance between supply and demand for energy-related products would prove to be a precursor to more important fundamental shifts in the economy triggered by the great inflation of the 1970s and the Fed's attempt to gain control over inflation and inflation expectations.

The Fed's third tightening cycle in just ten years, which began in 1987 and culminated into the 1990–1991 recession, was noteworthy because inflation dipped from just above 5 percent at the end of the decade toward the 2.5 percent area, where it has stayed ever since. This explanation of events gives rise to the belief that the Fed's efforts to contain inflation had created the benign inflation environment experienced in the early 1990s, especially when combined with the inflation-fighting efforts of other important central banks.

This interpretation credits the central bank's credibility with breaking the back of the wage-price spiral, but did the cyclical contraction orchestrated really change economic fundamentals enough to temper inflation? Our analysis of the events that coincided with the Fed's policy shift suggests that something more powerful came into play, which also explains why deflation risks are now the biggest policy concern.

Chapter 13

A Shift to Excess Supply

The central bank's credibility can be credited with tempering inflation in the early 1980s, but it cannot explain the breakdown in the Phillips curve evolving since the 1990–1991 recession. Neither can the central bank's credibility explain why the advanced economies have been struggling with a deflationary bias since the financial crisis in 2007. If central banks' credibility was the only factor at work in the push to reinflate by the Bank of Japan, and more recently, the European Central Bank, then the Fed would have proven effective in achieving the stated goal for returning inflation to a sustainable 2 percent trajectory. Instead, central banks continued to struggle against deflationary pressures. If their enhanced credibility is not the primary driver of the disinflation in Japan that began in the early 1990s, then something more fundamental is at work in the global economy. Specifically, our analysis suggests recent developments are a result of a shift in the global economy from a position of excess demand following World War II to that of excess supply. This fundamental shift began to become evident in the wake of the 1990 recession, and it became very clear during the deflation scare following the 2007–2008 financial crises.

This shift away from excess demand has also changed the nature of the business cycle. Prior to the 1990–1991 recession, the credit deterioration associated with recessions was simply a symptomatic development that affected a small collection of institutions instead of the broad-based systemic phenomena experienced more recently. The change in the nature of the business cycle evident in the data also includes the evolution of jobless recoveries and a lengthening of the business cycle upturns. These important changes in the nature of the last three postwar cycles support our more fundamental interpretation of these developments.

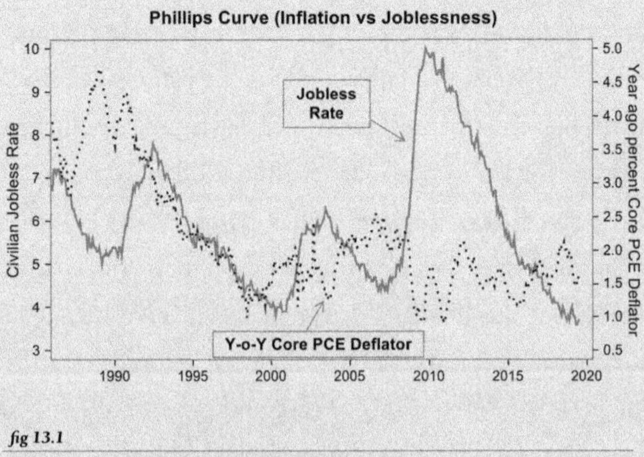

fig 13.1

Source: Macrobond, Mizuho Securities USA, BEA, BLS

Phillips Curve (CPI vs. Joblessness)

The 1990 cycle, for example, saw a collapse of the thrift industry and a contraction in commercial real estate–related banking. The 2001 recession was caused by a restructuring of nonfinancial sector liabilities, while the 2007–2009 recession saw a forced restructuring of the household sector's balance sheet and that of the banking industry. Specifically, a collapse in a speculative bubble in the residential real estate market triggered a collapse in the mortgage market, and in the subprime commercial paper market, that was further amplified by the associated liquidity crunch in the derivatives market tied to the origination process. This evolution in the business cycle, away from simple inflation cycles and toward credit-induced cycles, reflects a fundamental shift in the economy between demand and supply pressures.

The liquidity event that triggered the 1990–1991 recession was created by the Fed's desire to stem the tide of a modest rise in inflation before it could take root in higher inflation expectations. The resulting credit consolidation, however, took on a life of its own, and policy makers were forced to do more than just cut rates to get the economy moving again at a sustainable rate. Only after the nonperforming real estate–related debt was restructured, with government assistance, was the economy able to bottom and begin the process of recovery. This first credit cycle of the postwar period clearly shows that something fundamental was in the process of changing in the economy; but economists could not yet appreciate the importance of what we now know was the shift from excess demand to excess supply. This fundamental shift essentially requires policy makers, and more broadly, the economics community, to reconsider the tools necessary to implant policy decisions, as well as how policy addresses imbalances in the economy. What caused this shift away from excess demand toward excess supply was a combination of structural changes in the economy—especially the shift from defined benefit to defined contribution retirement schemes, the firing of air traffic controllers, and the development of the Internet.

The shift in retirement funding away from corporations to the individual was a huge development—the importance of which only surfaced over time and which is still influencing the economy today. Specifically, this shift in retirement funding initiated the institutionalization of wealth, and eventually the globalization of wealth. Both factors powered the rapid growth in the emerging economies and the financial innovations that revolutionized the way investments in new plant and equipment are funded. Developments in the emerging world had been a principal driver of the transition to excess supply, as these economies provided a ready pool of low-cost workers that could be employed to produce goods more cheaply than could be accomplished with domestic labor only. To compete, domestic providers had to innovate rapidly or go out of business. The net result had been the gradual development of excess capacity in most tradable goods markets.

The movement to defend a contribution retirement system was one of President Reagan's key policy initiatives, and it supported investment in the new labor-saving manufacturing process. As part of Reagan's supply-side tax cut, or the Economic

Recovery Tax Act of 1981, individual retirement accounts were promoted. In addition to phasing in a 23 percent reduction in the top marginal tax rate over a three-year period, to 50 percent from 70 percent, and cutting the capital gains tax rate to 20 percent from 28 percent, the Reagan tax cut advanced the president's desire to increase individual savings for retirement through the introduction of IRAs/401(k)s. The idea was simple, but it had far-reaching effects. By making individuals responsible for their own retirement, the Reagan team initiated a fundamental restructuring of corporate governance focused on generating double-digit returns for shareholders.

In order for an individual to save enough for retirement, they would need to earn double-digit returns on their investment. To achieve these high, sustained returns, companies were forced to focus on maximizing shareholders' returns through investment in labor-saving equipment to cut costs, and drop the added value to the bottom line. To ensure this trend was sustained over time, CEOs' pay began to be linked to gains in shareholders' value. To maximize shareholders' value, companies had to become mean and lean; cost cutting became an important driver behind corporate decision making, and it remains a key corporate focus today.

A strike by air traffic controllers in early August 1981 furthered the shift in corporate policy away from market share to maximizing profitability. In the first forty-five years after World War II, labor unions remained very powerful, and for a time, labor market stability was the key to a healthy economy, supporting the growth of union power. Strikes typically resulted in significant wage and/or benefit gains for workers, as company managers had confidence they could pass on the increased cost to consumers as well as the costs associated with lost output due to labor unrest—which was perceived as something worth avoiding. This view toward labor unrest made perfect sense in a world of excess demand and anchored inflation expectations. Unfortunately, inflation expectations did not stay well anchored, and the ability to pass increased labor costs to consumers eventually led to an inflation psychology that initiated the wage-price spiral that spawned stagflation. The combination of accelerating inflation and rising joblessness proved politically untenable, and policy makers had to react.

The Fed eventually broke the negative feedback loop between wages and prices by initiating the long, deep economic contraction of the early 1980s. Yet, it was the firing of the air traffic controllers by President Reagan that gave the Fed's new policy stance a real chance at success. PATCO workers were forbidden to strike against the government. When they opted to walk off the job on August 5, 1981, despite the president's warnings, the administration made good on its promise and fired any worker who took part in the strike. Despite the immediate disruption to air travel, the president's stand against a powerful union emboldened CEOs to take a stronger stand in their own labor disputes.

With the economy struggling in the wake of the Volcker tightening, CEOs looked to control their labor costs, and union givebacks became a reality, starting in the auto industry. This important manufacturing industry was reeling from new environmental/miles per gallon regulations and increased foreign competition. The dollar's surge in the wake of the Volcker tightening in the early 1980s and the exploding budget deficits increased foreign competition in all manufactured products, which limited the corporate sector's ability to pass price increases along to the consumer. The result was a decidedly more flexible labor market when President Reagan's term expired than existed when he entered the White House as a former union man himself.

Financial innovation touched off by the Volcker tightening also played a role in morphing the economy toward excess supply. In particular, the growth in high-yield and derivatives markets—such as interest rate swaps—introduced new avenues for companies to fund their investments in labor-saving plant and equipment. These new financial products complemented the investment incentives included in the Reagan supply-side tax cut. The spike in interest rates, which followed the Fed's shift from interest rates to money supply, targeted the deep recession that followed. It resulted in several companies losing their investment-grade credit rating. These so-called "fallen angels," or companies whose credit ratings dipped below a BBB rating, enhanced the liquidity in the high-yield market, given the familiarity investors had with the companies in this space. The increase in liquidity and the demand for double-digit returns by investors in a defined contribution world increased alternative financing sources for companies, especially start-ups that could not have obtained this financing prior to this cycle of innovation. The rapid expansion in financial markets generated by the institutionalization and globalization of wealth provided additional motivation behind the shift from excess demand to excess supply. At the same time, new derivative securities, which Wall Street began to generate, increased companies' willingness to borrow, as they allowed the issuer to hedge different aspects of the risks involved in being exposed to the debt markets.

The development of the personal computer, or PC, was a big factor enabling financial market innovation with the ability to manipulate large streams of data quickly and inexpensively, accelerating the pace of financial engineering. The increased access to inexpensive data processing allowed analysts to break up debt obligations into their component cash flows and reassemble them into new, customized obligations. The growth of the PC and the development of the Internet browser in the 1990s added a whole new round of investment spending, this time on new digital technology. These investments in technology built on the earlier gains from investments in new plant and equipment, which, over time, increased the efficiency of every industry, and is still changing the way products are produced and distributed in both the domestic and global economies.

These important developments have gradually shifted the economy to a world of excess supply, which is the only logical explanation for the current predicament central banks find themselves in today, and why their policies to date have not generated the results they anticipated. But before we get into this important discussion, it will be instructive to discuss the changed nature of business cycles that has occurred due to the shift in the balance between supply and demand.

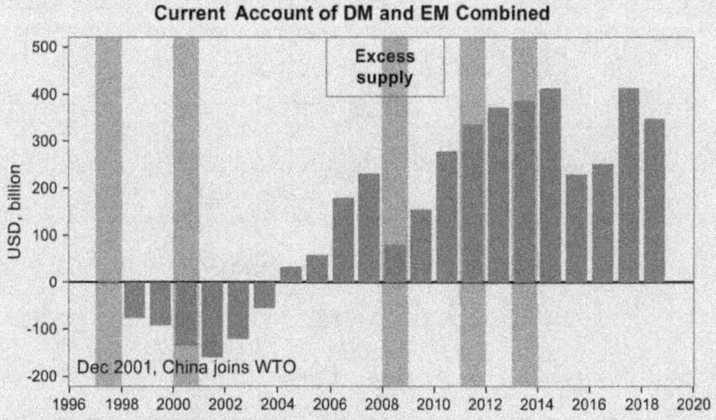

***fig* 13.2**

Source: Macrobond, Mizuho Securities USA

Current Account/Developed vs. Emerging

Credit vs. Inflation Cycles

Although the shift to excess supply from excess demand has clearly tempered the inflationary bias the economy experienced in the period immediately following the shift to a fiat monetary standard in 1971, there are other important changes in the nature of the business cycles that have resulted from this fundamental shift. In particular, business cycles have tended to be longer in duration as excess supply has become an issue. In fact, two of the more recent expansions have lasted more than ten years, including the one that began in July 2009, which is now the longest in the postwar period. The extended duration of upturns reflects not only the more benign inflation environment, but also the longer time it takes for excess to build up in the economy. With inflation no longer driving the business cycle, cyclical upturns continue until credit-related imbalances build in the economy. These can develop in several ways, but typically, it is an asset liability mismatch that triggers a liquidity event that results in a recession. Over-leveraged companies tend to shorten the duration of their liabilities, giving a positively sloped yield curve. This deteriorates credit quality, and as the cost of financing rises, investor risk aversion increases. As the cost of borrowing rises, the risk of default rises, and eventually, a liquidity squeeze is triggered, and the recession unfolds.

Of the eleven post–World War II business cycles, the first eight were clearly inflation cycles, and the final three were credit cycles. The difference between inflation cycles and credit cycles is whether the credit event associated with each cycle was symptomatic or systemic. The credit events change the nature of the recovery. Inflation cycles tend to be followed by a solid recovery phase, while credit cycles are followed by shallow recoveries. The first credit cycle was also followed by the first jobless recovery of the postwar period, which was experienced following the 1990–1991 recession. As mentioned earlier, the collapse of the thrift industry and the damage done to banks, which had significant exposure to commercial real estate, created a liquidity squeeze that was slow to release its grip on the availability to funding. Even though the Fed was aggressive in easing after it felt inflation pressures had been adequately suppressed, the recovery was slow in responding to monetary stimulus. In fact, it was the jobless recovery that was blamed for President George H. W. Bush losing to Bill Clinton in the 1992 election.

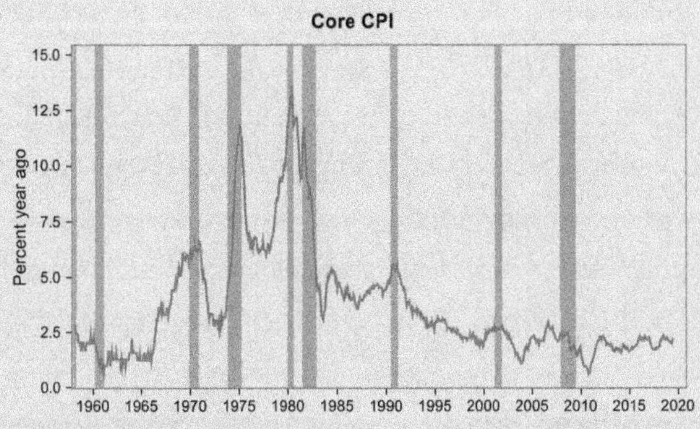

***fig* 13.3**

Source: Macrobond, Mizuho Securities USA, (BLS)

US Core CPI

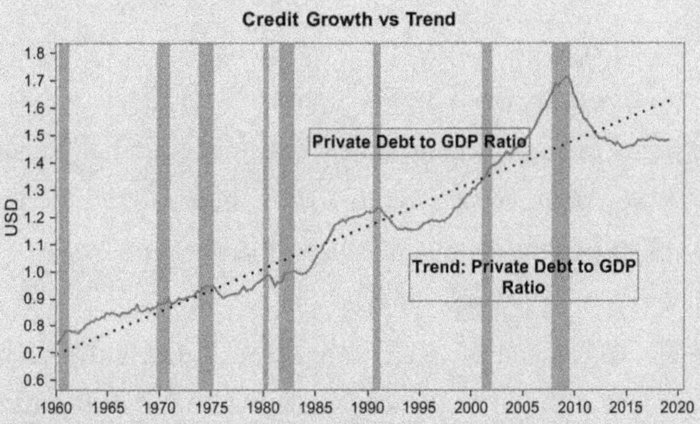

***fig* 13.4**

Source: Macrobond, Mizuho Securities USA, BEA, US Federal Reserve System

US Credit Growth vs. Trend

It took a full ten years for the next economic recession to occur. This exceptionally long expansion was the result of a lack of inflationary pressures building in the economy. With the shallow jobless recovery extending for several years, the gradual elimination of excess capacity kept a tight lid on both wages and prices just as new digital technology began lifting productivity in the economy. The so-called virtuous cycle, or support by an accommodative Fed policy of keeping rates low in the wake of benign inflation, helped extend the business cycle and inadvertently set the stage for the next systemic credit event. The steep curve that the Greenspan Fed orchestrated in the mid-1990s as an insurance policy against a premature recession over time resulted in an excessive reliance on short-term borrowing by nonfinancial corporations in the United States. This would prove to be the expansion's Achilles' heel. This low, short-rate environment also fanned the flames of the dot-com bubble that burst when the Fed eventually hiked rates, fearing a rise in prices could become a new sustained round of inflation. The major credit event associated with the 2001 recession was the collapse of the commercial paper market in the wake of the failure of Enron, WorldCom, and Calpine.

The eight-month-long 2001 recession lasted from March to November and was particularly shallow for a postwar business cycle. The mild nature of the cycle reflected the speed at which financial markets restructure the debt of companies caught in the cash-flow squeeze ignited by the Fed's tightening cycle that began in late 1998. This policy tightening pushed the funds rate up some 250 basis points to above 6.5 percent and forced corporate issuers to term out their debt rather than face increasingly illiquid short-term debt markets. Corporate malfeasance issues surfaced initially in the energy space but broadened out from there to telecom and other industries, where borrowing at the front end to finance long-term investments had become routine. Easing the way for this debt restructuring process was some 450 basis points in rate cuts executed by the Fed beginning in January of 2001 and completed before year-end, resulting in a 1.75 percent funds rate target. Reducing the severity of the recession further was the stimulus provided by the Bush tax cut, or the Economic Growth and Tax Relief Reconciliation Act of 2001, passed in the wake of the 9/11 terrorist attacks. This piece of legislation lowered the top marginal tax rate to 35 percent from 39.6 percent. The act also reduced capital gains taxes and increased pre-tax contributions for IRAs and other defined contribution plans.

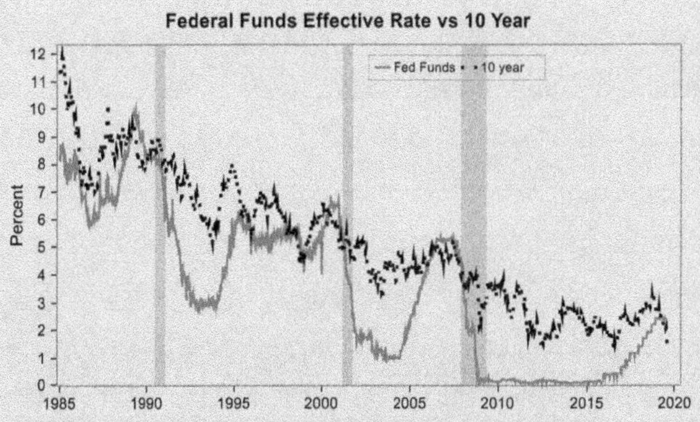

fig 13.5

Source: Macrobond, Mizuho Securities USA, Bloomberg, Federal Reserve Bank of New York, US Federal Reserve

Fed Funds vs. Ten-Year Treasury Note

The expansion that began in December 2001 proved to be the shortest of the three credit cycles of the postwar period, lasting just six years and one month. A noticeable lack of inflation experienced during the shallow recovery phase and the early expansion period prompted the Fed to continue pushing short rates down toward 1 percent and then hold it there until June 2004. This atypical Fed easing into the early stages of a cyclical upturn was then followed by a steady and preemptive tightening cycle designed to keep goods inflation under control even as asset inflation was accelerating. Rapid gains in home prices, which exceeded 15 percent in the 2005–2006 period for both new and existing homes, led to a rise in homeownership and excessive risk taking by individuals and money managers who saw the wealth being created as a self-sustaining process, until the bubble burst.

A gradual but steady Fed tightening that began in 2004 eventually pushed the funds rate upward to 5.25 percent from 1 percent over the course of a relative two-year period, flattening the important 2-year/10-year portion of the curve from over 275 basis points to near zero between late 2005 and mid-2007, before it became clear that the housing bubble was in the process of imploding. As short rates rose and the curve flattened, home prices plunged and so did the value of financial assets that were tied to mortgages. This negative feedback damaged the health of important financial institutions, several of which failed or needed government assistance. This list of tainted institutions included Bear Stearns, Washington Mutual, Merrill Lynch, AIG, and Lehman Brothers. The failure of Lehman Brothers would prove to be the largest bankruptcy in US history and created a systemic crisis-like environment rivaling that of the Great Depression.

To counter the crisis-like mentality triggered by the highly publicized events, the Fed pushed short rates to zero before expanding its balance sheet to fend off deflation risks and undertaking several special targeted liquidity initiatives designed to correct specific market failures. The recession associated with the financial crisis was deep and long. The contraction lasted eighteen months and saw the GDP output gap balloon out to 6 percent and the civilian jobless rate climb rapidly toward 10 percent. The contraction in growth and the liquidity crisis forced General Motors to seek an infusion of capital from the government, while Fannie Mae and Freddie Mac went into government receivership, where they remain today. These nontraditional policy initiatives created enough liquidity in the system that by June 2009, eighteen months after it peaked, the economy recovered; but again, the process was slow and short rates remained at near zero until December 2015.

Concerns over the Fed's desire to begin the process of slowing growth in its portfolio erupted in May 2013, pushing long-term rates upward by about 150 basis points, effectively doubling the yield on the 10-year note in just a few months. This so-called Taper Tantrum delayed any attempt at policy normalization until late 2015, when confidence in the economy, inflation, and financial markets increased enough to suggest that, gradually, rising short rates, a predetermined process of balance sheet unwind, would not jeopardize the improvement in conditions.

After nine rate hikes between December 2015 and December 2018 and about $800 billion in reductions in the Fed's balance sheet, the tightening process abruptly ended. The unwind clearly distorted the shape of the yield curve, as it was concentrated at the front end of the maturity spectrum, causing the Fed to reassess its normalization strategy heading into year-end. The flattening of the curve experienced during the run-up to the December 2018 rate hike reflected market expectations, which were not justified, that short rates would be hiked by another 100 basis points in 2019. This ramp-up in expectations caused a pronounced curve flattening and triggered a sharp sell-off in the equity market.

The curve flattening and equity sell-off that led to rising recession concerns among investors caused the Fed to surprise the markets heading into 2019 and signal a less restrictive stance than had been discounted by the markets. Despite this deterioration in growth expectations, it is important to note that the Fed's nine rate hikes undertaken since December 2015 failed to squeeze corporate or household cash flow. Specifically, the nonfinancial corporate sector kept the duration of its liabilities uncharacteristically long, while the household sector continued to deleverage a full ten years into an expansion. The fact that Fed rate hikes failed to dis-intermediate the economy is reflected by the economy logging one of its best growth years of the long expansion in 2018, rising by 2.9 percent, even though markets became increasingly unsettled. This divergence was also reflected in the behavior of credit spreads—the spread between corporate bonds and Treasury debt of a similar maturity—which remained exceptionally tight.

The highly unusual recession/expansion dynamics discussed above support the view that the nature of the business cycle has changed in the wake of a fundamental transition from excess demand to excess supply. Essentially, the length of expansions has increased; the recovery phase has become drawn-out and much more tempered from a growth perspective, or a jobless recovery. The nature of the recession has also changed, with the downturns tending to be deeper and requiring a more aggressive policy response from the Fed, Treasury, and congressional involvement.

Bank balance sheet restructurings were necessary in the wake of two of the past three recessions, and both were systemic in nature. The failure of the thrift industry in the early 1990s and the creation of the Resolution Trust Corporation (RTC) to warehouse nonperforming real estate loans depressed the banking industry. Less than thirty years later an even bigger debacle consumed the banking industry, beginning in 2007. The 2001 recession, on the other hand, was a forced balance sheet restructuring of the nonfinancial corporate sector. This forced restructuring was expedited by the aggressive Fed easing, which followed in the wake of 9/11, and the timely Bush tax cuts. This double dose of stimuli allowed companies to extend duration and reduce their risk of default in a concentrated period, eliminating the asset liability mismatch at the center of the credit crunch.

Revelations of corporate malfeasance prompted the credit squeeze that took on a life of its own, very quickly forcing companies to extend the maturity of their outstanding liabilities. The third credit cycle of the postwar period, experienced between 2007 and 2009, was a forced restructuring of both the household sector and the banking industry's balance sheets. This systemic collapse in both the banking and housing markets was triggered by a bursting of the housing bubble and the liquidity crunch that originated in the mortgage market and the derivative securities tied to mortgage debt.

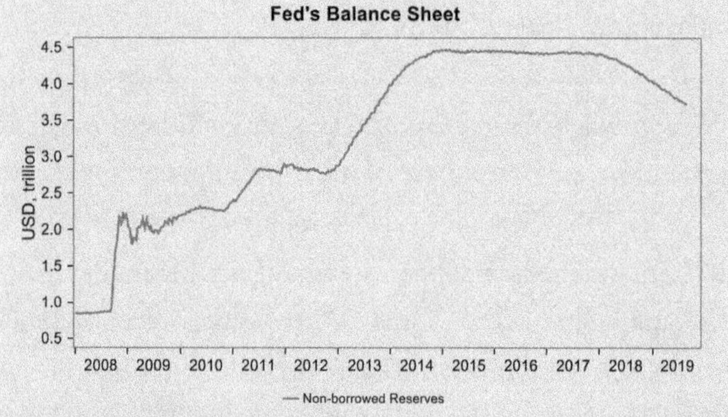

fig 13.6

Source: Macrobond, Mizuho Securities USA, US Federal Reserve System

The atypical nature of the last three business cycles is evidence of the shift in the balance between supply and demand in the economy. The factors behind the evolution from excess demand to excess supply described in this section provide a better explanation of why inflation has become more muted despite a fiat currency standard, record budget deficits, and the growth in the Fed's balance sheet. The central bank's credibility clearly played a part in the process of dampening inflation and inflation expectations in the 1980s, but it cannot explain the emergence of deflation in Japan and the recent slide toward deflation that has gripped Europe—nor can it explain why the Fed's attempts to reflate the economy have failed. The failure of the Fed to achieve its 2 percent inflation target despite having monetized almost $3 trillion in debt between August 2007 and January 2015 is clear refutation of the credibility argument.

The only logical explanation for these developments is a fundamental shift in the economy, rather than the role of money. More important, monetary policy needs to be reassessed, given the new excess-supply world. The aging of the population in the advanced economies is another consideration, suggesting that a new approach to economic analysis, and particularly the role of money in the economy, is in order. To address these issues, we will conclude this analysis by focusing on the possible role of inflation targeting and Modern Monetary Theory. Cryptocurrencies will be discussed, but their role in securing purchasing power in a world of deflation risks seems exceptionally limited and unnecessary.

Conclusion

What's Next?

The evolution of money, both in theory and in practice, reflects the ever-changing nature of the economy and that of individuals' preferences. Economic theory of money has basically gone through three distinct iterations in recent history, which we discussed in some detail in Section 1. There, chapters on Keynesianism, monetarism, and New Keynesianism provided different interpretations of how money and the economy functions.

Keynes's view of how the economy functioned contrasted with the classical school of thought, which dominated during the pre-Depression era. The classical school of thought claimed that in a world with fully flexible wages, prices, and interest rates, the economy tends to gravitate toward its natural rate of growth. Any disruption in the goods, labor, and money markets is quickly corrected by a series of automatic adjustments in three key endogenous variables: wages, prices, or interest rates. This means the supply and demand for money, like that of the overall economy, will always tend toward equilibrium. In the classical model there is little need for either fiscal or monetary policy, as disturbances either endogenously or exogenously induced will automatically be corrected by the system's innate flexibility.

Keynes expanded on the classical model by introducing sticky wages and prices in the general framework of the economy. This modification helped Keynes explain the extended disequilibrium that emerged in the late 1920s and early 1930s—the Great Depression. Keynes's interpretation of the workings of the economy created a place for fiscal and monetary policy to help correct disturbances in the system. The extreme social cost of the Depression led Keynes to view fiscal policy as the principal policy lever, suggesting that monetary policy was to be used to support the policy agenda of an elected government.

The Changing Role of Money in Economic Theory

The application of Keynesian fiscal policy intervention in the 1950s and 1960s was an attempt to tame the business cycle, leading to stagflation. Policy makers tried to exploit the perceived trade-off between joblessness and inflation, as suggested by the Phillips curve, in order to maximize employment at the expense of a little extra inflation.

The rampant inflation of the late 1970s and the politically unacceptable stagflation environment of the early 1980s led to the second interpretation of how the economy functions. This time, the economics community adopted a model based more on empirical analysis as the driver of theory. This reassessment was based on the long-term correlation between money-supply growth and inflation championed by economists like Milton Friedman. The empirical work undertaken by the monetarists also showed that there was no long-term effect between money growth and the real sector that could justify an attempt to smooth out the business cycle. As such, there was no exploitable long-term trade-off between money growth and the economy, or, more specifically, between the jobless rate and inflation.

The monetarists' interpretation provided a straightforward answer for why the Phillips curve proved to be vertical in the long run even if it was positively sloped in the short run. The ideal monetary policy suggested by this alternative view is to target a rate of growth in money that is consistent with an acceptable level of long-term inflation. Well-anchored inflation expectations will keep interest rates low and maximize employment, given the underlying pace of real growth determined by trend population and productivity growth. This policy framework supported the Fed's decision to abandon its interest-rate-targeting operating procedure in 1979, and instead, to target money supply. By limiting the growth of reserves in the banking industry, unhinging the federal funds rate from monetary policy, and linking it directly to the supply and demand for reserves in the banking system, the Fed could temper inflation and allow the economy to generate maximum employment in the long run. This policy prescription fit perfectly with both rational expectations and the inflation expectations–adjusted Phillips curve envisioned by the monetarists. By adding inflation expectations to the trade-off between unemployment and inflation, a vertical long-term relationship could be modeled, and stagflation explained.

The Fed's experiment with money-supply targeting resulted in dramatically higher short-term interest rates. This increase in rates triggered financial innovation and eventually caused the empirical link between money and inflation, at the center of the quantity theory of money (QTM), to break down. This important link was severed by the introduction of interest-paying alternatives to checking accounts. These innovative financial products blurred the lines between savings and transactions balances. Initially, there was an attempt to reestablish this link by targeting alternative monetary aggregates, but the inclusion of additional liabilities in the money-supply target only added more savings balances, and the transitions component became a less important driver of money-supply growth. Instead, household and corporate portfolio decisions began to determine the level of money demanded in the economy. As the trends in inflation and money supply diverged, the Fed was forced to shift back to a modified interest-rate-targeting operating procedure advocated by the neoclassical economists.

The third and more recent school of economic thought, New Keynesianism, is rooted in the micro foundations of macroeconomics, and explains involuntary unemployment as workers' rational assessment that the benefits of searching for a better job outweigh the costs of forgoing employment at a lower wage. This interpretation of how the economy works sees the business cycle as the result of unexpected shocks to the system, which can affect either aggregate supply or demand. These shocks can be either positive or negative, depending on their source, and can temporarily push the system out of equilibrium. It is this economic model that allowed the Fed in the 1990s, under Chairman Alan Greenspan, to let the economy run hot despite inflation fears as new digital technologies began boosting productivity and dampening inflation pressures. As deflation pressures accumulate globally, however, it is beginning to be reflected in domestic conditions and presents a fundamental challenge to the preemptive/gradualists' approach to monetary policy that has guided the Fed since the mid-1990s. Today's challenge is the mirror image to that which forced Chairman Volcker to boldly alter the course of monetary policy in late 1979 and adopt monetarism. Today's deflation risks present an equally challenging dilemma for the Fed.

As discussed in Chapter 13, the new risks confronting the economy stem from a fundamental shift from a position of sustained excess demand to that of excess supply. This critical transition can be explained by the supply-side revolution initiated by President Ronald Reagan, who looked at the domestic economy in the late 1970s and early 1980s and recognized that demand-side management was not having the effect expected by economists. He correctly saw that the economic and social problems created by inflation could be corrected by expanding the supply side of the economy rather than limiting demand. Although simple in concept, his supply-side revolution was exactly the right approach, and was truly visionary. Many of the policies he championed, such as a supply-side tax cut, were designed to boost investment spending, but they proved of little value long-term, as they were quickly reversed when political pressure mounted for reining in runaway budget deficits. However, the shift from defined benefit to defined contribution retirement schemes and his firing of the air traffic controllers kicked off a series of developments that helped transform not just the domestic economy, but also the global economy, in the wake of the institutionalization and globalization of wealth. The digital revolution initiated by his Star Wars approach to defense spending and the support for the Internet by technology-savvy politicians like Senator Al Gore and technology companies all worked to achieve today's highly efficient and dynamic global market for tradable goods at the heart of the excess supply world and global deflation risks.

The supply-side revolution was slow to materialize, but when China joined the World Trade Organization in 2001, the transition shifted into overdrive. The benefits of lower prices were quickly evident, but the costs associated with this economic imbalance only surfaced in the wake of the 2007–2009 recession. The global financial crises that erupted in 2007 and lasted into 2009, and severely depressed aggregate demand, set the stage for deflation in a world of fiat currencies. This development is something that current economic models struggle to explain and economists never expected, in a world where money is no longer tied to gold.

The risk of runaway inflation through currency debasement and devaluation was the risk policy makers feared and attempted to guard against at Bretton Woods; this had repeatedly surfaced throughout history whenever monetary discipline was relaxed. Deflation, on the other hand, was believed to be the result of an undesired and/or an ill-advised contraction in money, like that which preceded the Great Depression. A ballooning central bank balance sheet and the printing of money is supposed to be inflationary, suggesting that the shift to excess supply is the only logical reason for this unexpected macro development. The transition from symptomatic to systemic credit debacles independently supports the shift to excess supply and explains why new approaches to economic theories such as Modern Monetary Theory and the introduction of cryptocurrencies are being explored by policy makers and investors, even though neither is likely to go mainstream.

REVERSING DEFLATION IS PROVING DIFFICULT

Policy makers have launched several initiatives that have proven to be ineffective in countering deflation. Japan, for example, has struggled with deflation since the early 1990s, and repeated attempts to reverse this adverse economic development have failed in the last thirty years. Even the recent three-arrow approach launched under Abenomics has failed to reverse the deflation that has gripped the country for three decades. Abenomics and its three-step program advocated by Prime Minister Shinzo Abe included monetary easing, fiscal stimulus, and structural reforms. Unfortunately, a lack of significant structural reform and/or meaningful fiscal stimulus appears to have left Japan struggling with deflation, even though there was some evidence that the central bank's aggressive easing under Bank Governor of Japan Kuroda was starting to boost prices.

Europe is also struggling with deflation pressures in the wake of the sovereign debt crisis that erupted in 2009 when Greece, Portugal, Spain, and Cyprus were unable to repay or refinance maturing debt obligations. Faced with the threat of the euro region breakup, Mario Draghi, president of the European Central Bank, unleashed his last salvo of stimulus to "do whatever it takes" to defend the common currency. With large-scale asset purchases already in place, his new initiative was a special low-cost borrowing program called TLTROs, for countries facing a liquidity squeeze. Although this program provided much-needed liquidity to the system and the crisis mentality dissipated quickly, it did not, however, correct the broader banking system's troubles at the heart of Europe's economic problems. The contraction and anemic economic recovery that followed in the wake of the sovereign crisis compounded the lingering problems facing Europe in the wake of the global financial meltdown, allowing a deflation psychology to begin taking root on the continent and reflected in negative long-term interest rates.

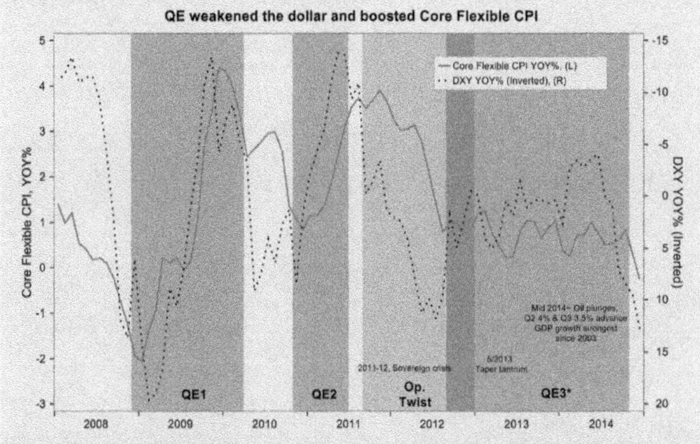

fig Conclusion 1

Source: Macrobond, Mizuho Securities USA, Atlanta Fed, ICE

QE and the Dollar

Deflation pressures that took root in Japan thirty years ago, and more recently in Europe, have yet to become evident domestically. However, the risks of importing global deflation have not gone ignored by domestic policy makers. The Fed countered the global financial crises with a series of novel policy tools, including cutting short rates to zero; using forward guidance to manage interest-rate and inflation expectations; large-scale asset purchases; and targeted liquidity programs designed to address funding problems unique to certain markets and/or market participants. The important contrast between the way policy makers addressed the 2007–2009 financial crises in the United States relative to Europe is the emphasis put on correcting the banking systems' imbalances. Europe has yet to complete its restructurings ten years after the crises. This is reminiscent of the way Japan dragged its heels back in the 1990s, when the bubble economy burst. Unresolved banking system problems acted as a weight on the economy and limited the ability of monetary and fiscal policy to support the economy. Although restructuring bank balance sheets is necessary to avoid a deflationary spiral, it is not sufficient, especially in a world of excess supply. It is not, on its own, enough to ensure that deflation is avoided. A coordinated policy response like that envisioned by Keynes is the best approach. Moreover, the Fed's recent experiment with quantitative easing shows nontraditional policy still works when interest rates are no longer effective and can be used to combat deflation. Expanding the Fed's portfolio to over $4.25 trillion from about $800 billion between 2008 and 2015, the Fed successfully lifted both inflation and inflation expectations. Unfortunately, the Fed's later attempts at managing the shape of the yield curve by manipulating the composition of its balance sheet and then trying to normalize its balance sheet offset the benefits of its earlier efforts. This left the domestic economy vulnerable to global deflation pressures.

The Next Evolution in Theory?

We explored the long, rich history of money being linked to gold in Section 2, as well as the costs and benefits of relaxing the discipline imposed by gold in order to better manage the business cycle. We have examined how shifting to a fiat currency model came with the risk imposed by delinking money from gold. In fact, the stagflation experienced in the early 1980s reflected worst-case fears of those who argued against adopting a fiat currency in the 1970s, many of whom still long to return to gold. The adoption of money-supply targeting suggested by economists like Friedman can be viewed as imposing discipline to a fiat currency model. Although the empirical link between money and inflation broke down in the late 1980s, the Neo-Keynesian method still emphasized a disciplined approach to policy by emphasizing the Fed's long-term goals of containing inflation as the key to achieving maximum employment.

A key underlying assumption of the theoretical and practical role in the economy presented in this analysis is that the economy is operating under excess demand, but this critical assumption is no longer valid. As a result, the economic models that economists have come to rely upon no longer adequately explain how the economy functions. Policy decisions based on these models have not yielded the desired results. This, in turn, has led to a search for alternatives to the more traditional approach to policy and levers that can be exploited to influence real growth and the labor markets. The recent growth in the popularity of Modern Monetary Theory (MMT) is a clear example of the failure of more traditional macro models to predict recent adverse economic developments like stagnant wages, increased income inequality, and accumulating deflation risks.

MMT is the result of the failure of Neo-Keynesian economics to predict deflation under a fiat currency standard. The search to provide an adequate response to the adverse social consequences of a lack of pricing power in the economy has led to increased interest in alternative economic policies like MMT. Although the quantity theory of money advocated by Friedman and implemented by Chairman Volcker was an economic model based on empirical analysis, MMT is based on basic Keynesian analysis and the developments in Japan over the last thirty years and more recently in Europe and in this country. Much like monetarism, MMT is based on a simple intuitive assumption about the nature of the link between money and the economy; but instead of it driving inflation, this theory holds that monetizing the debt can be used to increase real growth without increasing default risk. The idea is simply that a government that borrows in its own currency can never default, and that the risk of inflation is an acceptable risk relative to the benefits of a stronger economy.

According to this interpretation of how the economy works, money is a public monopoly managed by the government. Unemployment is seen as evidence that the currency monopolist is overly restricting the supply of financial assets needed to pay taxes and satisfy desired savings. A key assumption behind this theory is that money originated with governments attempting to direct economic activity and not out of the need to speed transactions in an economy. The value of money in a fiat currency world is generated by the fact that it can be used to pay taxes owed to the government. Essentially, MMT is a modern form of chartalism and is sometimes referred to as neo-chartalism. MMT advocates argue that the government should use fiscal policy to achieve full employment by creating more money to fund government purchases. Accordingly, the primary risk once the economy reaches full employment is inflation. Raising taxes and issuing bonds to remove the excess money from the system should address this side effect of overstimulus.

A fiat monetary regime is seen as an essential element underlying the MMT model. Specifically, when a government issues its own money, this model states that a government—

1. Can pay for goods, services, and financial assets without the need to collect taxes or issue debt
2. Cannot be forced to default on debt denominated in its own currency

3. Is limited in creating money only to the extent that it generates inflation
4. Can control demand-pull inflation by eliminating excess money in the system by taxes or debt
5. Does not need to compete with the private sector for savings balances by issuing debt

The first four of the above are basic tenets of MMT and are basically in agreement with traditional economic theory; however, the fifth is not. MMT asserts that issuing debt does not crowd out private investors because it simply cancels out another government obligation—money supplied to the system. The theory behind MMT asserts that because a government can issue its own currency at will, the level of taxation relative to government spending is a policy tool that regulates inflation and unemployment—it is not a means of funding its activities. This aspect of MMT is a direct contrast to the austerity approach advocated by other macroeconomic theories. More to the point, government spending and taxing decisions are the primary means of achieving full employment. Governments need to establish a level of the deficit, which is consistent with achieving this objective.

Cutting interest rates is also seen as ineffective in a slump because weak profits and reduced sales expectations limit spending decisions, so fiscal policy is needed to boost demand. Additionally, cutting interest rates is seen as a negative, since it reduces government spending.

The mechanics of MMT are straightforward: The Treasury

sells directly to the Federal Reserve a zero-coupon perpetual and deposits the money printed to buy the bonds directly into the Treasury's account at the Fed. The administration then spends the money to increase aggregate demand and reduce joblessness. This theory is clearly a shift back to fiscal stimulus over monetary policy and can be viewed as a return to Keynesianism, but without the long-term restriction of balancing the budget.

Whether policy makers will adopt MMT is an interesting question, and one that should not be easily dismissed. Social pressures to correct the imbalances created by deflation may not build as slowly in this country, or in Europe, as they have in Japan. Moreover, history suggests that deflation is a very difficult condition to correct—it was only the outbreak of the war in the 1940s that ended the last global deflation imbalance created by the Great Depression. Japan's thirty-year struggle to break deflation's grip on the economy and Europe's recent slide into negative rates all suggest deflation is once again spreading among developed countries. There is evidence to suggest that even China is susceptible to accumulating deflation risks. Deflation is insidious, in that it leads to high real returns even as nominal yields decline, increasing the real cost of paying down debt outstanding. This then depresses economic activity and generates stagnant or declining wages and rising unemployment.

Moreover, the destruction of wealth triggered by deflation eventually creates a sense of urgency to do something to correct this abnormal situation. The more policy makers feel the political pressure to exit a deflationary spiral, the more likely they are to try something as unorthodox as MMT. For a democratic government, the allure of being able to ramp up fiscal stimulus could eventually outweigh the risks and uncertainties attached to adopting a policy that is clearly questionable in nature for short-term political gains. A growing sense of hopelessness surrounding policy makers' ability to reverse deflation will add to the call for drastic and perhaps unorthodox action.

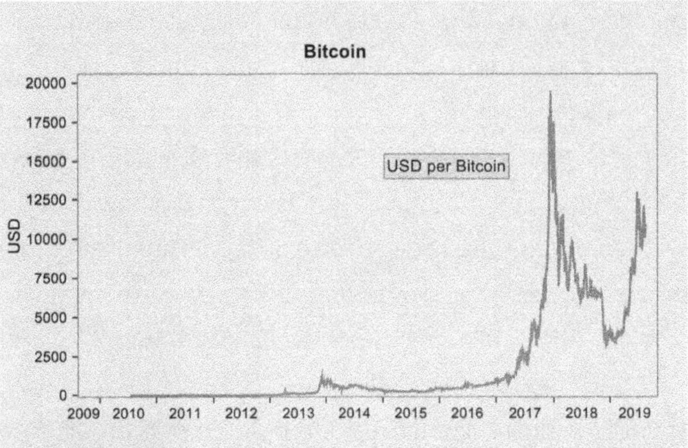

fig Conclusion 2

Source: Macrobond, Mizuho Securities USA, US Federal Reserve System, ECB, BOJ

Bitcoin Price Since 2009

The Next Evolution in Practice?

The other interesting recent development regarding money is the introduction of cryptocurrencies, which is a clear pushback against the lack of discipline imposed by a fiat currency model even as MMT is being discussed. Cryptocurrencies are digital assets designed to work as a medium of exchange. These digital currencies now number over 4,000 and use strong cryptography to secure the transactions, control the creation of additional units, and verify the transfer of assets. More important, these digital currencies use decentralized control, in contrast to the digital payment systems established by traditional financial institutions and central banks. The decentralized control of each cryptocurrency works through a distributed ledger technology, primarily blockchain, which serves as a public transactions database.

The first true cryptocurrency was Bitcoin. It was launched in 2009 by an unknown person or group using the name Satoshi Nakamoto; it was released as open-source software. Bitcoins are created through a process called mining, which is designed to limit the creation process—in other words, to impose discipline. The more expanded the network becomes, the more difficult and, therefore the more expensive, it becomes to generate new coins. Besides creating an anonymous payment system, which resides outside the traditional financial system, and where transactions can be made only with the use of unique computer keys, the mining process limits the creation of new coins.

The important point behind the explosion in cryptocurrencies since 2009 is that this coincides with a period when central banks, including the Fed, were in the process of dramatically expanding their balance sheets and in the process printing money. The fact that the generation of new cryptocurrencies is almost unlimited, as currently evidenced by the diversity in digital currencies available, reduces the value of this alternative to traditional money as a means of eliminating currency debasement. But it does highlight that there is still a desire among individuals and investors for currency that maintains its value over time to serve as a store of wealth.

GENERALLY ACCEPTED DEFINITION OF A CRYPTOCURRENCY

1. The system does not require a central authority; its state is maintained through distributed consensus.
2. The system keeps an overview of cryptocurrency units and their ownership.
3. The system defines whether new cryptocurrency units can be created. If new units can be created, the system defines the circumstance of their origin and how to determine ownership.
4. Ownership of cryptocurrency units can be proved exclusively cryptographically.
5. The system allows transactions to be performed in which ownership of the cryptographic units is changed. A transactions statement can only be issued by an entity proving the current ownership of these units.
6. If two different instructions for changing ownership of the same cryptographic units are entered simultaneously, the system performs, at most, one of them.

One Last Thing

The important point that should be obvious now is that money is central to the workings of the economy, and that its role has evolved dramatically over the course of time and is still evolving today. The ever-changing role that money plays in the economy also means that policy makers need to continuously evaluate the tools they employ and the intermediate objectives that they set.

Failure to recognize the important changes that have evolved in the economy has twice in the last seventy-five years led to truly unexpected economic developments as policy makers misread the economic conditions they faced. The first big policy failure of the postwar period was the stagflation experienced in the late 1970s and early 1980s. When it was finally addressed, it required a spike in short-term interest rates that would accelerate financial innovation and trigger a chain of economic developments that contributed directly to the second major policy failure—the financial crises of 2007–2008. The global deflationary bias that followed in the wake of the financial system meltdown of the Great Recession has created an even more difficult dilemma for policy makers, as evidenced in Japan's thirty-year struggle with deflation.

To properly address this new situation, economists and policy makers need to come to grips with the basic fact that we now live in a world of excess supply, and that the role of policy is no longer controlling the rate of inflation, but ensuring that inflation hits a target that avoids deflation, even in the face of a recession. Key to targeting inflation in a world of excess supply is the central bank's balance sheet; interest rates are not the key policy tool. The other key to addressing the new world of excess supply and deflation is recognizing that business cycles are now tied to the evolution of the credit cycle. This means recessions will tend to be deeper and recoveries slower, requiring a bigger inflation cushion to avoid the risk of deflation from becoming entrenched in the system. With the United States as the world's largest net debtor nation, deflation would be a worst-case scenario. Luckily, fundamental changes such as this do not happen that often—once every thirty-five to forty years or so; but when they do, policy makers need to be ready to execute radical changes in their reaction function, or they will become part of the problem, not the solution.

About the Author

Steven Ricchiuto has worked on Wall Street since 1980, as an economist, strategist, and director of fixed income research. He worked at several firms prior to joining Mizuho Securities USA LLC, including Donaldson, Lufkin & Jenrette; Kidder Peabody; and Dean Witter. He also worked in the US securities arms of several European banks, such as Barclays; ABN Amro; and Svenska Handelsbanken. He is currently the US economist at Mizuho Securities USA LLC. His latest two books are *Disequilibrium: How America's Great Inflation Led to the Great Recession* and *Symptomatic to Systemic: Understanding Postwar Cycles and Financial Debacles.*